Crazy Laws
and Lawsuits

A "Dungeon" Barbie doll complete with a rubber bondage dress and helmet did not appear to violate the copyrights of Mattel, the judge concluded.

By an odd quirk of the law in Cambridge, England, the university was permitted to run its own prison.

Two daughters who were "distressed" sued the hospital for letting them see doctors rush to help their mother.

A mother sued a furniture store after tripping over a toddler. The toddler turned out to be her own son.

An airline had to pay $2 million to its passengers who suffered 28 seconds of turbulence...

... it is illegal in Florida for women to fall asleep under a hair dryer...

Crazy Laws and Lawsuits

A COLLECTION OF BIZARRE COURT CASES AND LEGAL RULES

Robert Allen

Sterling Publishing Co., Inc.
New York

Library of Congress Cataloging-in-Publication Data Available

2   4   6   8   10   9   7   5   3   1

Published by Sterling Publishing Co., Inc.
387 Park Avenue South, New York, NY 10016
© 2005 PRC Publishing
Distributed in Canada by Sterling Publishing
c/o Canadian Manda Group, 165 Dufferin Street
Toronto, Ontario, Canada M6K 3H6
Distributed in Great Britain by Chrysalis Books Group PLC
The Chrysalis Building, Bramley Road, London W10 6SP, England

Printed in Malaysia

Sterling ISBN 1 4027 2495 0

Contents

Introduction

This book started life as a bit of fun. Everybody knows about crazy lawsuits and many people enjoy whiling away a bit of spare time swapping stories about them. The person who comes up with the most amazing case earns the admiration of friends. For reasons we will go into later, the majority of really odd lawsuits come from America. So, for Americans there is a subtext that says, "Oh my God, just look what's happened now!" and for other nationalities the subtext is, "Just how crazy are those Yanks going to get?" This keeps everybody happy.

Or does it? One of the pleasures of being a writer is that you get to inform your audience of something you know more about than they do. The subtler, and more valuable, pleasure is that you get to know more about the subject while you are writing. The thing I learned while writing this book is that lawsuits are just not funny. They may look funny if you are standing at a safe distance. So do fireworks. But get up too close and in both cases you stand to get badly burned.

Crazy lawsuits have a number of consequences that are not remotely funny. The first is that people who are honest, decent, and doing nothing but trying to get on with their lives are frequently dragged before the courts and ruined financially because they had the bad luck to fall foul of some idiot with a hard luck story and a sharp lawyer. You'll find plenty of stories like that in these pages and, to speak plainly, they stink. Because you tripped and spilt hot coffee on someone's lap, do you deserve to be sued and reduced to penury? Should you be ruined because someone's kid cycled in front of your car, leaving you no time to brake (and you really weren't going fast)? People with common sense would say "no" but common sense is going out the window where the law is concerned. As Charles Dickens' Mr. Bumble put it, "...the law is an ass, a idiot." And it's got a lot worse since his day.

> As Charles Dickens' Mr. Bumble put it, "...the law is an ass, a idiot." And it's got a lot worse since his day.

What else is wrong with our litigious age? First, there is the waste of public money. Every time someone sues the city and wins a couple of million dollars that is money that the city could have used for something useful like schools or hospitals. It also wastes the time of the legal system. Courts that are crammed with stupid lawsuits are not getting on with their proper business. They are wasting the time of highly-trained and highly-paid professionals by making them concern themselves with nonsense. But then, of course, not all those highly-paid professionals mind—because now we come to the lawyers. There was a time when most middle-class parents would have aspired to getting one of their kids into the legal profession. Nowadays they'd probably rather the kids robbed a bank. At least bank robbers are good plain crooks.

> Is it really a coincidence that numerous crazy lawsuits are brought by people in prison?

It is breathtaking the sheer hatred and venom that many Americans now direct at lawyers. Any American can tell you lawyer jokes and lawyer horror stories. Only the jokes aren't really that funny because they refer to a once dignified and important profession that has been brought down by greed and stupidity. It is tragic that someone who has been extensively and expensively educated in the law can then use that training in the most cynical way to extract rich rewards from the misfortune of fellow citizens. Whoever first came up with the concept of "no win, no fee" should really rot in hell. At one time, going to the law was an expensive business that was a last resort in an attempt to right genuine wrongs. This was bad in its way because it meant that the law belonged to those who had enough money to use it to their advantage. But democratization of the law has been a disaster because it allows people to misuse it to make money. It also provides an outlet for those who have too little to do with their lives. Is it really a coincidence that numerous crazy lawsuits are brought by people in prison? It must help to while away those idle years and may even provide a nest egg for when they are released.

But the very worst thing crazy lawsuits have done is to convince people that they are not to be held responsible for their actions. No matter how stupid, misguided, immoral, or downright criminal those actions may have been, they were always someone else's fault. And that "someone else" has to be made to pay. Is this really the lesson we want our kids to learn as they grow up?

There are other downsides to the lawsuit situation. For example, teachers have become less willing to take classes on educational trips. Why? Because they know that if the slightest thing were to go wrong they could get sued and lose their livelihood. A few years ago I was involved in arranging regular trips for kids who wanted to visit New York. I was supposed to go along as one of the chaperones but, for various reasons, had to refuse. The trip I was supposed to accompany was led by a colleague who, to protect the innocent, we'll call Sam. He was the deputy principal of a high school and had thirty years' experience in teaching, during which time he'd escorted countless school trips. He took this group of kids to New York, showed them around, and made sure they all had a great time.

On the journey back, one of the girls approached him and told him that, in spite of the rules and warnings the kids had been given, she and one of the boys had had sex and now her period was late. Sam was completely floored by this news. He and the other chaperones had done everything they could to avoid this happening but, of course, unless you chained the kids to the walls of single-sex dungeons, there was no way you could monitor their every move. In any case, this was supposed to be a holiday and so they had to be allowed some freedom. Sam viewed the end of his career—when his local newspaper got hold of the story, (with the subsequent publicity for him and his family)—with feelings of terror you can easily imagine. It eventually turned out that the girl had been "joking." Did Sam see the funny side? No, he simply vowed that he would never, ever lead another school trip. He stuck to that decision and, what's more, no other chaperone stepped forward to take his place. So now a lot of kids who would have enjoyed a chunk of the Big Apple will not be able to do so.

The problems in schools do not stop here. Children are now increasingly being forbidden to take part in activities that their parents took for granted. Skipping has been banned in some places, snowballing and making ice slides are both out, throwing balls around is far too dangerous, and, of course, running is just bound to end in a fall and possible legal action. So kids are being taught to be inactive, but, at the same time, we are worried about them getting fat partly because they take insufficient exercise.

> The sad truth is that stupid and unnecessary litigation is not purely an American phenomenon.

The sad truth is that stupid and unnecessary litigation is not purely an American phenomenon. It may have started in the states but, like Coca Cola or McDonald's, it is rapidly becoming a truly international brand. If you view British TV nowadays, you will see frequent ads placed by firms of lawyers who offer "no win, no fee" services. The voice-over murmurs persuasively,

"Have you been involved in an accident that wasn't your fault? Phone us today and we will tell you instantly whether you have grounds for a claim." Since advertising on TV costs megabucks you can be sure that the lawyers are already doing brisk business.

This trend is all the more surprising when you remember that the Americans consider themselves a robust and independent nation and the Brits congratulate themselves on the wisdom, common sense, and fairness of their legal system. How could these down-to-earth folks allow themselves to go down such a slippery slope? To my utter amazement, there are even crazy lawsuits in Australia. The Aussies are the plainest, bluntest, most commonsensical folks on earth. If even they are becoming infected with legal fever, we are surely doomed.

> The plain truth is that people don't have to sue. Why not take some responsibility for what happens to you?

There are, however, some rays of hope, even in the U.S. In California, there is an organization called the Citizens Against Lawsuit Abuse (C.A.L.A.) that campaigns against frivolous lawsuits. There is also the American Tort Reform Association

(A.T.R.A.), an organization with similar aims. They are responsible for publicizing a lot of these lawsuits and drawing attention to the damage they cause. Keep up the good work!

The plain truth is that people don't have to sue. Why not take some responsibility for what happens to you? When George Bush got a pretzel stuck in his throat and nearly choked to death, did he sue the makers? No, he admitted it was a dumb thing to do and that his mother had always told him to "chew before you swallow." In this, at least, people might learn to follow his example and not see every tiny mishap as a chance to make a killing.

The other thing that we learn from lawsuits is that some people are just plain stupid. They cannot get their heads round some pretty simple propositions like, "If you eat junk food all the time, you will become obese," or "If you put your dog in the microwave, it is going to die." There have always been dumb people around, but until recently they were mocked for their stupidity—now they get a lawyer and sue. More judges and juries need to have the guts to say, "You've been stupid so put up with the consequences and go away."

Here is an illustration of just how worried Americans are now about being sued. William Bronchick, who describes himself as a "best-selling author and attorney," runs what he calls his Wealth Protection Boot Camp. The boot camp is advertised on Bronchick's web site and its stated aim is to, "Discover how to Protect Yourself, Your Business and Your Family from Lawsuits, Taxes & other Financial Disasters!" He also tells you, "Your odds of being sued are greater than your odds of being in the hospital!" If you're not already scared, you soon will be. Bronchick goes on to inform you:

"IT'S NOT A MATTER OF IF, IT'S A MATTER OF WHEN! Lawsuits are another everyday threat to your financial well-being. Imagine a thug sticking a .357 magnum up to your throat and demanding you turn over your wallet, credit cards, jewelry, and keys to your luxury car. How do you feel? Scared out of your mind? Vulnerable? Violated? You will feel exactly the same way (and maybe worse) when you are hit by a lawsuit and you know you haven't done anything wrong! I will teach you the skills you need to protect yourself from being a target for the "bloodsuckers" and "ambulance chasers." With impenetrable walls of protection around you, lawyers and greedy plaintiffs won't be able to touch you or your assets!"

Finally, it is necessary to say a few words about the lawsuits themselves. First, it is true that because crazy lawsuits are often related as funny stories, some people have started to make up their own fictional cases. There is a boom market in urban legend lawsuits. At first, I worried that we might unintentionally spread false rumors. Reports of lawsuits are usually at least secondhand and sometimes they have been recycled and embroidered many times over. However, there are plenty of lawsuits for which you can find reliable sources. Many have been picked up by reputable news agencies and others have been quoted with reference to court records. Often the ones for which we have best authority are even crazier and more bizarre than the ones that are told over a couple of beers and usually start, "There was this one guy..." So take some of what follows with a tiny pinch of salt. But just because some of the cases are fictional, don't be led to assume that they all are or that frivolous litigation isn't a serious problem.

Chapter One: Odd Laws

Don't look at me that way

You may not think of New Yorkers as being too genteel. They usually have the reputation of being direct to the point of rudeness. So it may come as a surprise that there is an anti-flirting law in force there. If you get caught looking at a woman "in that way," you can be fined $25. If caught a second time, the offender can be made to wear a pair of blinkers to curb his offensive activity.

Adequately bearded

There is little amusement to be had from contemplating the Taliban regime that, for a while, ruled Afghanistan. They enforced the Islamic Shariah law with great ferocity. Whippings, beatings, amputations, and stonings were routine. Only in one respect did they produce an unintentional touch of humor. The law required that not only should all men have beards, but that they should not trim their beards. Before the Taliban, it had always been considered that the proper length for a beard was so it might be grasped with one hand. This was not good enough for the zealots who decreed that each of their officials should go equipped with a lamp glass. If a person was suspected of having inadequate face fungus then the beard would be inserted into the glass and if no hairs appeared at the far end there would be trouble. Even given the nasty character of the Taliban regime, it is hard not to smile at the thought of grown men solemnly inserting their beards into a lamp glass.

Confined in Cambridge

By an odd quirk of the law in Cambridge, England, the university was permitted to run its own prison. This was not, of course, intended for the young gentlemen who studied there. Their crimes and misdemeanors were punished in a much less drastic way. The prison was reserved for prostitutes who, in the opinion of the authorities, were guilty of offering their services to students. Arrest and imprisonment were quite arbitrary and any young woman who attracted suspicion could find herself whisked away and locked up for as along as it took to teach her the errors of her ways. For many years this custom continued without attracting any public criticism, but eventually the authorities went too far. One day a charabanc-load of London milliners visited the city which, even in the 19th century, attracted many day-trippers. The young women were alarmed to find themselves rounded up and put behind bars. When the facts of the case became known, there was at last a public outcry and this ancient and barbaric practice was discontinued.

Loss of horsepower

London's famous black taxis are the direct descendants of the horse-drawn hackney coaches. As the internal combustion engine gradually replaced horse power as the means of travel in the city, the laws governing public transport were slow to catch up. As a result, long after all taxis were powered by a diesel engine, it was still a legal requirement for drivers to carry a bale of hay to feed the horse.

The emperor's clothes

In China, the color yellow was forbidden to everyone except the emperor. Almost everything around him was yellow, from floor tiles and dishes, to even his pillow cases and blankets. The last emperor, P'u Yi was kept away from other children until the age of seven, when finally he received a visit from his brother and sister. The children played together and all was well until he noticed that the lining of his brother's sleeve was yellow. He was absolutely furious until his brother tactfully explained that the color was not imperial yellow but apricot.

Lèse-majesté

Thailand is known as "the land of smiles" and most of the time this is quite true. However, the unwary visitor can end up in trouble by not observing local customs. For example, you should never touch somebody on the head, or sit with the sole of your foot pointing at another person. These are simply customs and any transgression will probably earn you no more than dirty looks. However, the law that forbids lèse-majesté (an offense against a sovereign) is still rigorously enforced. Nor is it just a matter for the lawyers—even members of the general public react furiously to any insult offered to the royal family. Even today, the musical The King and I is banned because it shows King Mongkut in a ridiculous light.

Some years ago, a British tourist was doing a little souvenir shopping when the shopkeeper offered him a rather garish portrait of the queen. He took one look and said, "No thanks. That's a terrible picture!" The girl, who spoke little English, thought he was criticizing the queen rather than the picture and immediately ran outside and summoned the police. The unfortunate tourist was fined heavily for his disrespect.

Occasionally, cases of lèse-majesté get completely out of hand. Back in the 1970s, some radical students hanged the crown prince in effigy. Fellow students who witnessed the crime were so incensed that they seized some folding chairs that lay handy and used them to beat the offenders to death.

I can't believe it's not butter!

In the Canadian province of Quebec, margarine and butter must be different colors—it's the law! This is because a powerful lobby of dairy framers worried that margarine, a cheap and cheerful butter substitute, was starting to resemble the real thing. This was not a trend they welcomed. Eventually the government decreed that margarine should be dyed a rather nasty shade of red. This caused widespread revulsion and for a while no one would eat margarine at all. A compromise was finally reached and margarine began to be produced in a very pale shade of yellow.

Loose moose

Many years ago in Fairbanks, Alaska, the guy who owned the
local bar got himself a pet moose. The unusual pet soon
developed a liking for alcohol and both the bar owner and his
customers would ply the animal with beer until it got
completely drunk. The rest of the population didn't find the
moose's antics so funny because it would stagger out of the bar
and wend its drunken away along the town's sidewalks to the
considerable inconvenience of other pedestrians.

It is no surprise, therefore, that the town introduced a local
ordinance forbidding moose to walk on sidewalks. Why they
didn't have a law forbidding people to give animals beer is
not recorded.

The wait is killing me

When is a murder not a murder? This question exercised some
of England's greatest legal minds for some considerable time.
What, for example, if you got into a fight and hit someone who,
though injured, did not die straight away? Supposing that
person died much later, could the assailant be tried for murder?

Eventually, a rule was introduced that set the time limit at a
year and a day. Anyone whose injury resulted in death within

that period might be considered to have been murdered. If you injured someone and they survived for longer than that time, you were in the clear.

Beware oncoming cows

What is so odd about a law that states, "No cows may be driven down the roadway between 10 am and 7 pm unless there is prior approval from the Commissioner of Police?" Only this: it is a local law contained in the Metropolitan Streets Act of 1867, which refers specifically to London. Any cow loose on the city's streets, with or without permission, would very soon be steak.

Making the punishment fit the crime

In England, it used to be against the law to commit or attempt to commit suicide. The maximum penalty? Death.

Iron clad law

In the U.K., it is against the law for a Member of Parliament (M.P.) to enter the House of Commons wearing armor. This dates from the days of Charles II, who became king after the death of Oliver Cromwell. Both King Charles I and the Lord Protector (as Cromwell was known) had been in the habit of using military force in an effort to control the decisions of the House of Commons (the legislative house). This law was designed to put a stop to such attempts. For similar reasons, the monarch is not allowed to enter the House of Commons. When the Queen's Speech is read at the beginning of each new parliament, the M.P.s have to troop into the House of Lords to listen to it.

This law stinks!

Down in Tennessee, they take their skunks seriously. The law states: "It is unlawful for any person to import, possess, or cause to be imported into this state any type of live skunk, or to sell, barter, exchange or otherwise transfer any live skunk, except that the prohibitions of this section shall not apply to bona fide zoological parks and research institutions." So should you fancy going south for a weekend break, take our tip and leave the skunk at home.

Dueling danger

Picture the scene: you're traveling through West Virginia and stop for coffee and a snack at a roadside cafe. While quietly enjoying your coffee, two men sitting nearby get into an argument and one of them challenges the other to a duel. Instead of stepping outside to settle the dispute in Clint Eastwood fashion, the challenged man yells, "Don't kill me! I'm too young to die!" and rushes for the door. At this point do not, whatever you do, yell after him, "There goes the yellow streak." If you do, you will be breaking a law that states: "If any person post another, or in writing or in print use any reproachful or contemptuous language to or concerning another, for not fighting a duel, or for not sending or accepting a challenge, he shall be guilty of a misdemeanor, and, upon conviction, shall be confined in jail not more than six months, or fined not exceeding one hundred dollars."

See weed? Leave it be!

You'll need a lot of self-control to avoid breaking this law. You know how we all like to go out at night and collect a little seaweed? It's a pleasant habit and, you would have thought, harmless enough. But not, it seems, in New Hampshire where for some reason, there is a law against it. The law states: "In Night: If any person shall carry away or collect for the purpose of carrying away any seaweed or rockweed from the seashore below high-water mark, between daylight in the evening and daylight in the morning, he shall be guilty of a violation." So now you know. However tempted you may be, remember, just say "No."

Improperly dressed to kill

If you find yourself in New Jersey with murder on your mind (and, let's face it, why else would you consider going there?), make sure you are properly dressed for the occasion. It's bad enough that you are going to commit homicide, but if you do it while wearing a bullet-proof vest you will be in very serious trouble indeed. Here's what the law has to say: "A person is guilty of a crime if he uses or wears a body vest while engaged in the commission of, or an attempt to commit, or flight after committing or attempting to commit murder, manslaughter, robbery, sexual assault, burglary, kidnapping, criminal escape or assault."

It had better be butter

Should you be passing through Wisconsin and stop for a snack, you should look very carefully at the butter on your roll. Could it be that you have been duped into accepting margarine instead of real butter? Call a cop! The law states: "The serving of colored oleomargarine or margarine at a public eating place as a substitute for table butter is prohibited unless it is ordered by the customer." There's far too much of this sort of thing going on. Do your public duty: have the café owner jailed right away.

This must be a yolk!

You remember in Gulliver's Travels there was a war between those who opened their eggs at the big end and those who preferred to open them at the little end? Swift probably thought that this was a bit of wild satire that was too ludicrous to be true. Wrong. In England and Wales, there was a law dating from the time of Edward VI that said: "Any person found breaking a boiled egg at the sharp end will be sentenced to 24 hours in the village stocks."

Drowsy but dry

Should you find yourself in Florida and feel the need to visit a hairdresser, you should not be too surprised if the staff behave a tad strangely. Once you're under the drier, you may find that they ply you with cups of strong black coffee, or even give you the odd surreptitious kick on the ankle. Why? Because it is illegal in that state for women to fall asleep under a hair drier and, should you get caught, not only you but the salon owner will be fined.

Fair play

Should you be in Arizona and have the misfortune to be attacked by, for example, a knife-wielding assassin, be careful what you do. If you draw a knife of your own and stab him to death, you'll be well within your rights. But should you be foolish enough to pull a gun and shoot him, you will be in deep legal trouble. The law in that state asserts that when being attacked by a criminal or burglar, you may only protect yourself with the weapon that the other person possesses.

Drink driving

The Scots have always had a love/hate relationship with alcohol, which from time to time has led to rather strange behavior. For example, not that long ago, there was a law that allowed pubs to open on Sunday evening but only for the benefit of genuine travelers. The result was that every Sunday people would jump in their cars and drive just far enough to reach a place where they weren't known. They would then get in a jolly evening of drinking before walking a little unsteadily back to their cars and driving home. Quite why the authorities thought this was a good idea was never explained.

It was this same genius for pointless regulations that led to a rule that anyone buying methylated spirits (denatured alcohol) had to sign the poisons book. This was to prevent the practice among down-and-outs of buying "meths" (denatured alcohol), mixing it with cider or cheap wine, and drinking it. This meant that respectable housewives, who used the stuff for cleaning, were solemnly made to sign the book. It seems to have occurred to no one that many alcoholics, though homeless, were quite capable of signing their names.

Jus primae noctis

Jus primae noctis means "law of the first night." It is widely believed that in medieval Europe, there was a law that allowed the local Lord to take the virginity of all the young women within his domain. What is curious is that there is no proof that such a law ever existed. It is almost certain that aristocrats would have used their power to enjoy themselves with young woman over whom they had control. No one has ever found it written down anywhere, yet most people have heard of it and believe that it existed.

Reverse graffiti

This is not so much an odd law as an odd way of getting round a law. A graffiti artist in the north of England was fed up of being accused of vandalism. He wasn't one of these young kids who try to plant their "tag" in unusual places—he was a proper artist who wanted the freedom to express himself. He felt that his work was beautiful and made a positive contribution to the community. The authorities were not inclined to agree. He mulled his problem over and came up with an ingenious solution. He made a series of stencils and then went out looking for the dirtiest walls in town. It didn't take long to find walls disfigured by years of grime. Our talented hero then taped his stencils to the grimy walls and cleaned them! When the stencils were removed his pictures appeared as islands of clean stone shining out of the sea of filth. Could cleaning a dirty wall (albeit selectively) be classed as vandalism? Surely not?

Christmas shoot-out

In Britain, Christmas has had a sporting connection for hundreds of years. Even now, as soon as the turkey and mince pies have been given a decent send-off, people turn their attention to sporting events. Boxing Day, the day after Christmas Day, is particularly known as a time for sports. But this has not always been so. In 1541, Henry VIII had a law introduced called the Unlawful Games Act which forbade all sports at Christmas with the notable exception of archery. The country's archers were the Tudor equivalent of a Weapon of Mass Destruction. They were greatly feared by enemies (i.e. the French) and with very good reason. So archery had to be practiced constantly, even at Christmas. Later, men were also allowed to indulge in "leaping and vaulting" at Christmas, in order to remain fit and strong.

Walk, don't drive

The short and inglorious reign of Edward VI is usually passed over without much comment in the history books because the writers are much more interested in getting to the exciting bits about his sisters, Mary I (Bloody Mary) and Elizabeth I (Good Queen Bess). Edward was a sickly boy who survived fairly briefly after ascending the throne. He did, however, introduce one law that is, at least in theory, still on the statute books. He decreed that everybody had to walk to church on Christmas Day. Why he found time to pass such a law when he did hardly anything else is a mystery. However, for his own good reasons, he had the law passed and people who now drive to church had just better watch out. It may be that finding a parking space will be the least of their problems.

Prosecuted pig

There are numerous cases throughout the history of laws that permit animals to be prosecuted for a criminal offense. For example, in 1386, a pig went on trial in Falaise, France, accused of having torn the face and arms of a child who later died. The pig was found guilty and was sentenced to have its head and forelegs mangled and then to be hanged. They dressed the pig in men's clothes and executed it in front of the city hall. The cost of the execution was recorded as "ten sous and ten deniers." The hangman was rewarded with a pair of gloves.

Pick of the day

As you probably know, the laws of the Jewish religion are many and complex. To follow them to the letter, as some choose to do, takes a huge amount of effort and has the effect of setting the ultra-Orthodox apart, not just from gentiles, but from their fellow Jews. It is not surprising then that in Israel there is a constant battle between those who would like to see all the laws enforced publicly and those who take a much more relaxed view of the matter. One outcome of this is that certain journalists who are of the relaxed persuasion have taken to investigating obscure points of law and asking religious leaders for their opinions. What they hope for is to find examples of really odd laws that will make the whole ultra-Orthodox position look stupid. This is how someone came up with the question, "Is it OK to pick your nose on the Sabbath?" No doubt they were hoping that nose-picking would qualify as work and be forbidden to the faithful. They were, however, disappointed. Apparently you can be as Orthodox as you like and still pick your nose whenever you want.

What's in a name?

When Napoleon Bonaparte overran much of Europe (especially Germany and Poland) he found that he was master of areas where there were significant Jewish populations. He introduced a law that required Jews to adopt "proper" European names. This idea had been kicking around since the French revolutionary government had ordered it in the late 18th century. Now there are two versions of the story and two parties who swear that theirs is the truth. You can believe either: version a) the Jews were allowed to choose names and, if they refused, a name was chosen for them, or version b) that unscrupulous officials made the Jews pay for their new names and gave out good names to those who paid most and stupid names to those who could afford least. Whichever version you believe, the fact is that names such as Goldstein, Rosenberg, Zuckerman, etc, are not really Jewish in origin but only by adoption.

There is another element to this story that you may find interesting. Why, you may wonder, do so many Jews have the Scottish name Ross? The answer is that it is actually a German name and comes from the poetic word for a horse. The English translation would be "steed."

More hedgehog, anyone?

If you're a driver, you won't go far without seeing road kill strewn across the highway. Foxes, hedgehogs, snakes, dogs, and cats are just a few of the creatures that get slaughtered by the traffic. You might even come across the odd pheasant that took off a split second too late. What do you do if you see a dead pheasant with no owner? Would you take it home for dinner?

I'm told that the bruising caused by the impact with a vehicle ruins the meat. But in any case you might consider eating it. You probably have no such thoughts when you see all the other bloodied corpses on these routes.

However, if you live in West Virginia, you might want to think again. In that state, the law specifically allows you to take road kill home for supper. So that's something to look forward to now, isn't it?

Beard bother

It is said that in Brainerd, Minnesota, every man is obliged to grow a beard. The law is, of course, out of date and it is unlikely that many of the inhabitants realize that they are dangerous lawbreakers. There was a time when it was customary for British sailors to grow a beard. It is said that when a young recruit wasn't keen on acquiring this badge of manhood, he went to see the Chief Petty Officer and asked him whether wearing a beard was compulsory. "No lad," said the CPO kindly, "you just mustn't shave."

Bath time

There is a law in Kentucky that you must take a bath once a

year. Unkind outsiders insist, jokingly, that far from being an example of an odd, obsolete law, it is one that Kentuckians stick to rigorously.

Cowboy case

You might be tempted to think that the law has gone crazy only recently but you'd be wrong. Back in the days of the Wild West, there was a lot of ill-feeling directed at people who used a newfangled device called "barbed wire" to protect their land. Wire fences were frequently cut and, in Texas, the problem became so acute that a law was passed making it illegal to carry pliers that could be used for wire cutting. There is a story that a cowboy was found to be carrying pliers and was taken before the local Justice of the Peace (J.P.). He protested that he hadn't cut any wire fences. The J.P. replied, "That may be so, but you were equipped for it so you're guilty." The cowboy replied, "Then why don't you have me arrested for rape as well?"

It's a dog's life in Oklahoma

In Oklahoma, dogs must have a permit from the mayor if they want to congregate in groups of three or more on private property. On the other hand, they do get some protection from the law. Anyone who makes ugly faces at a dog can be arrested and fined or jailed.

Puddle play

If most of the odd laws seem a bit straight laced, here's one from California that will warm your heart. Community leaders passed an ordinance that prohibits anyone from attempting to stop children from playfully jumping over puddles.

Crossing in Connecticut

The citizens of Connecticut live under a terrible legal burden: they are not allowed to cross the street while walking on their hands. As if this weren't enough to cope with, they are also expressly forbidden from biking at over 65 mph.

Sober in Kentucky

In parts of the U.S., there are some pretty strict laws about alcohol but in good old Kentucky, you are legally sober until the point where you "cannot hold onto the ground." If this sounds like their attitude to law and order is a little too relaxed, they make up for it with their draconian ice-cream legislation that makes it illegal to transport an ice cream in your pocket.

Lip service in Louisiana

You wouldn't think that Louisiana, famed for its southern charm, would need a law dealing with biting people but you'd be wrong. What's more, the law is not as straightforward as you might suppose. If you bite someone with your own teeth, you get charged with simple assault, but if you bite someone with false teeth that counts as aggravated assault.

Criminal callers

If you happen to be planning a bank heist or similar mayhem in Washington, you must be sure that you comply with the rules or you'll be in big trouble. Not only can you be charged with the crime you committed, but you will find that you are in violation of a strict city ordinance that requires you to stop at the city limits and telephone the chief of police before you enter town.

Smelly bits

It's surprising how many laws there are dealing with the subject of unpleasant smells. In West Virginia, for example, children are not allowed to go to school with their breath smelling of wild onions. While in Indiana, you are not allowed to go to the movies, attend a theater, or ride in any public vehicle until at least four hours after you have eaten garlic. On the other hand, bathing in the winter in Indiana is prohibited.

Harmless amusements?

You'd think that people would be allowed to play a few simple games to pass their idle hours, wouldn't you? But you have to be very careful. In Alabama, for instance, it is illegal to play dominoes on a Sunday. However, if you rush to Alabama looking for amusement, make sure that you don't get caught playing cards in the street with a Native American or you'll be in real trouble.

Bear behavior

In Alaska, you are allowed to shoot a bear, which is just as well since they can be very dangerous. On the other hand you are definitely forbidden to awaken a sleeping bear so that you can take its photograph. I have no idea what sentence the law imposes, but I'd bet that as far as the bear is concerned there can only be one penalty—death.

Unholy laughter

If you go to Alabama on a Sunday and feel like attending a church service, you'll be made very welcome—unless, that is, you happen to be wearing a false moustache with the intent of causing laughter, in which case you'll get arrested. Still, things could be worse. Had you been caught spreading salt on railroad tracks, you could be sentenced to death.

Caught in California

A lot of people shake their heads and mutter that California is "different." Certainly it is when it comes to hunting animals. For example, it is illegal to shoot game from a moving vehicle unless you are shooting a whale. If you are in Pacific Grove, you must be careful not to "molest" butterflies unless you fancy paying a $500 fine. And, of course, should you wish to set a mousetrap, you must not dream of doing so without first acquiring a hunting license.

Road rage restrained

If you are ever tempted to indulge in fits of road rage, make sure you stay well away from Idaho and especially from Pocatello where it is prohibited for pedestrians and motorists, "to display frowns, grimaces, scowls, threatening and glowering looks, gloomy and depressed facial appearances, generally all of which reflect unfavorably upon the city's reputation."

Illicit in Illinois

Getting into trouble in Chicago is simply a matter of opening your mouth. If you speak English, that is. According to city ordinances, you are only allowed to speak American. But if this seems odd then you should see some of the other local laws. For example, you are not allowed to fish in your pajamas or take a French poodle to the opera.

Armed and dangerous in Missouri

Let's face it, there has always been something a bit odd about Kansas City. For a start, why isn't it in Kansas? What the heck is it doing in Missouri? But the craziness doesn't stop there. In Kansas City, children are allowed to buy shotguns. And if you think that's lunacy, wait for the best bit—they are specifically forbidden to buy toy cap guns.

Noses in New York

When was the last time you greeted anyone by placing your

thumb against the tip of your nose and wiggling your fingers. When you were in kindergarten perhaps? If you ever feel like resuming this form of greeting, make darn sure you are not in New York where it is specifically forbidden.

Tippling in Texas

In Texas, the whole Encyclopedia Britannica is banned because it contains detailed instructions for home-brewed beer. In Lefors, the drinking rules are particularly strict—you are not allowed take more than three sips of beer while standing.

Chapter Two:
Ouch, That Hurts!

Wrist wrench

A woman went jogging wearing her Nike trainers. What could possibly go wrong? Well, she somehow managed to get her shoelaces into a tangle and fell over. O.K., bad stuff happens, right? Wrong! The woman was an orthopedic surgeon and when she fell, she suffered a permanent injury to her right wrist. This meant that her ability to carry out operations was, she claimed, permanently impaired. So what do you think would compensate her for a damaged career? She filed suit in the State of New York—seeking $10 million.

A grave affair

Do you remember the bit in the movie Carrie where her hand suddenly shoots out of the grave and grabs her friend? I bet that made you jump. But that was just one of those Stephen King stories, it could never happen in real life. Could it? Well, not exactly but Dorothy VerValen had an experience that was hardly less disturbing. She went to the cemetery to tend her grandfather's grave. Just as she went to clean moss off the headstone, the ground gave way and her right foot struck the coffin. Her left foot remained above ground but this placed it under such a strain that the ankle broke. Fortunately, help was at hand in the shape of Mrs. Ver Valen's daughter who helped to pull her free.

Now, there is a lawsuit pending. Mrs. Ver Valen is suing the city of Sultan, Washington. She wants compensation for her injuries, emotional distress, and legal costs. Her attorney says that the city authorities are well aware that older graves are prone to sinking, but that they haven't done enough to correct the problem. The city's lawyer counters with the argument that the cemetery is a public place, accessible 24 hours a day, and that the city can't be held responsible for every inch of all the public places under its control. It seems certain that it will be quite some time before this argument is laid to rest.

A swift exit

A family on vacation were driving along happily in their camper when their teenage son, who had been asleep, started to sleepwalk. He opened the door and stepped out quite oblivious to the fact that they were doing 65 mph at the time.

Miraculously he was not seriously injured. Even so, his parents decided to sue the manufacturers of the camper on the grounds that they should have provided a more secure locking system.

Bird bystanders

One day, Janice Bird was brought into Los Angeles County Hospital by her grown-up daughter, Nita, for outpatient surgery. After Mrs. Bird had been with the surgeon for about 90 minutes, there were complications and the procedure started to go wrong. Just at that moment, another of Mrs. Bird's daughters arrived. The two daughters saw the doctors hurrying to give their mother emergency treatment. They then saw Mrs. Bird being rushed down the hallway. Apparently, she had turned bright blue and her body was at a steep angle so that her head was almost touching the ground.

The amazing part of the story is that the daughters sued, not because of the medical treatment their mother received, but because they had had to witness it. The case dragged on and eventually found its way to the California Supreme Court where it was thrown out.

Bothered by bars

Two women were carrying some heavy burglar bars when one of them (the one who owned the bars) dropped them on her foot. She alleged that her helpful neighbor caused the accident. The neighbor was not too worried because she was insured and her insurance company offered to pay the injured woman's medical bills. The woman was not satisfied. She decided to sue and get damages for the "pain and suffering" she had endured.

The jury was unsympathetic and threw the case out. The neighbor, however, was forced to spend almost $5,000 in legal costs.

Adelaide action

A teenager from Adelaide, Australia, is suing his mother. He suffers from cerebral palsy and claims that the fact that his mother crashed into a tree while he was a fetus had a bearing on his condition. The mother, Sylvia Neave, is said to have been negligent and breached her duty of care toward her unborn child. As the law stands, the 16-year-old has to sue his mother and the third-party insurer to gain a $3.5 million compensation. Also included in the suit is the Queen Elizabeth Hospital which allegedly failed to treat him "sufficiently early or not at all."

Bruised by boobs

When Bennie Casson went to P.T.'s Show Club, he was expecting a little fun watching the striptease. What he didn't expect was that he was about to get hit round the head by a pair of massive boobs. According to his later statement, as reported in the St. Louis Post Dispatch, one of the strippers slammed her boobs into his neck and head region after he got a little too close for comfort. Susan Sykes, the dancer (whose stage name is Busty Heart) apparently had a chest measurement of 88 inches. The sudden impact of her outsize boobs left Mr. Casson with a "bruised, contused, lacerated" neck. He decided to sue because he had been caused, "emotional distress, mental anguish, and indignity." He was hoping to claim $200,000 in compensation.

Club catastrophe

Kara Walton of Claymont, Delaware, went out for an evening's socializing and ended up at a nightclub in a nearby city. However much she enjoyed the club, she decided not to pay the $3.59 cover charge. How was she to get out of paying? A bright idea came to her. She went to the ladies room and tried to climb out of the window. She was obviously not as agile as she thought because she slipped and fell to the floor, knocking out two of her front teeth in the process. Of course, you know what comes next. She sued the club and won $12,000, plus her dental expenses.

Coors of death?

Like a lot of these cases, this one starts out simple and ends up crazy. In 2002, 19-year-old Ryan Pisco of Reno, Nevada went to a party, had too much to drink, and was doing 90 mph in his girlfriend's car when he hit a light pole and died. Ryan's mother filed a suit against Coors Brewing Company on the unlikely grounds that their advertising had not sufficiently stressed the dangers of driving while under the influence. Well, there's a surprise! Note to J. Pisco: advertising is meant to emphasize the benefits of the product, you have to work out the downside for yourself. In the case of alcohol, the perils are not exactly a state secret.

Where this case gets really screwy is that Ryan's mother also sued his girlfriend and her mother. Apparently, Ryan was not a qualified driver and so it must have been his girlfriend's fault that he drove her car. And it must have been her mother's fault because she gave her a car. There's some fine logic at work here. Just perhaps Mrs. Pisco might take the time to reflect that that she should have warned her son against the perils of getting drunk and driving dangerously. If she had, she might still have a son and not a lawsuit.

Damaged doodah

There some things you wouldn't wish on your worst enemy. For example, Edward Skwarek left Canada for a nice relaxing vacation in the U.S.A. Everything went fine until he decided to enjoy a coffee at a Starbucks in Manhattan. At this point you may be yelling, "Not another of those 'hot coffee in the lap' stories!" Oh no, this one is much, much worse.

Edward decided that he needed to use the toilet. He was sitting comfortably, waiting for nature to take its course, when he turned to take some toilet paper. At this point the seat shifted. He leaned forward to correct his position and then the seat clamped his penis against the bowl. He is now suing Starbucks for $1 million claiming permanent injuries to his manhood. His wife is claiming $500,000 for the loss of his husbandly services.

Dangerous dancing

When Linda K. Powers, a dental hygienist from Georgia, went out for an evening's dancing she wasn't expecting it to end in physical injury. However, when Mike Lastufka offered her a dance, she accepted willingly enough. Mike decided to show off his best moves, so he attempted something he later described intriguingly as a "shag-style spin move." Apparently, he failed to pull it off, because it resulted in Linda falling and breaking a finger. She sued and an Atlanta jury awarded her $220,000 in compensation. According to reports, up to that point, the highest pay out in Georgia for a broken finger was $20,000. It's doubtful whether breaking this particular record was much comfort to Mike.

Dangerous diving

Would you dive into the shallow end of a swimming pool? No? "Too dangerous," you'd think to yourself. However, Steve Burrows, a guest at Missouri's Ramada Inn, didn't agree. He dived in—and broke his neck. He sued the hotel on the grounds that there was not adequate warning that such a dive was dangerous. It was eventually revealed that not only had Mr. Burrows been drinking before the incident but that the hotel had posted warning notices. This was not enough to convince the court and so the plaintiff was awarded damages of $3.9 million.

Now you'd think that Mr. Burrows' accident was the sort of thing that happens only very rarely. You'd expect to go for years without coming across another shallow-end diver. But you'd be wrong.

Mr. and Mrs. Shaw, a retired couple, took a brief vacation and, while they were away, their granddaughter invited a friend, Joseph O'Sullivan, round to swim in their pool. Guess what he did? Yes, that's right, he dived into the shallow end and fractured a cervical vertebra. So then he sued the Shaws. Unsurprisingly the case was thrown out. Even in America, there are some cases where common sense prevails. Undeterred Mr. O'Sullivan took his case to the Supreme Court where it was also thrown out.

Drain drama

If you've ever suffered from blocked drains, you may know about Liquid Fire. It's a liquid drain cleaner and, like all such fluids, it is highly caustic. A man in Georgia bought some and was worried that the container looked a bit flimsy. He was not convinced that it would be strong enough to hold the liquid safely so he had a bright idea: he would pour the liquid into a "safer" container of his own. When he did so, the contents spilled and he suffered excruciating burns and damage to his flesh. So, naturally, he is now suing the makers of Liquid Fire on the grounds that he was forced to carry out this dangerous maneuver because of his lack of confidence in the original container.

Drunk and litigious

A man was so drunk while driving that he swept past detour signs at high speed and crashed his car. Anyone who feels that he got what he deserved is not living in the present century. The man sued everyone he could think of. This included the firm that designed the road, the contractor who built it, a host of subcontractors, and the state highway department which owned the road. The case took five years to settle and eventually the plaintiff accepted an offer of $35,000. The engineering firm ended up having to pay $200,000 in legal fees.

Fat flyer

Philip Shafer from Ashland, Ohio, took a flight from New Orleans to Cincinnati. He was less than amused to find that he had been seated beside someone who, to put it plainly, was fat. No, we're not talking just a bit fat, we're talking the American equivalent of a sumo wrestler. Shafer later stated: "He was a huge man. He and I [were] literally and figuratively married from the right kneecap to the shoulder for two hours." What the folks at Delta may not have known when they devised the seating plan was that Mr. Shafer is a lawyer. He filed a suit seeking compensation for the "embarrassment, severe discomfort, metal anguish, and severe emotional distress" he had suffered. He reckoned that Delta owed him $9,500 in damages.

Full Moon

For anyone who doesn't know already, mooning is the practice of pulling down your pants down and giving your audience a full view of your bare behind. Now this may not be very sophisticated fun but in some circles, especially among students, it is regarded as the last word in robust humor. However, mooning has its dangers. Take, for example, the case of a college student in Idaho who decided to moon one of his friends from the window. In the excitement, he lost his balance and fell backward out of the window. He then decided to sue the college on the grounds that it had not provided students with adequate information about the dangers of falling out of windows.

How do you like my hairdo?

If you're married, you'll know that moment when your wife bursts through the front door in a fit of rage and gives you hell because her new hairdo has gone wrong. Then she dashes upstairs and spends half an hour in front of the mirror trying to fix it. Eventually, she re-emerges from the bedroom having decided that she likes it after all. Not all these incidents come to such a happy ending.

Geremie Hoff from St. Louis was so infuriated by what had been done to her hair that she sued the salon. She had gone to the Elizabeth Arden Salon to have her hair straightened. Apparently, the stylist applied a hair relaxer before washing and styling Mrs. Hoff's hair. She went home happy enough but, according to her testimony, that night clumps of hair started to drop out leaving bald patches. Mrs. Hoff was so upset by her changed appearance that she became depressed and required counseling. So bad was her depression that she took early retirement from teaching and stopped working as a tour guide. The court awarded her $6,000 in damages.

In a bit of a pickle

This is one of those cases that gets stranger as it goes along. It starts with a woman working in a convenience store in Charleston, West Virginia, who strained her back as she tried to open a pickle jar. Now, we've all had our moments of frustration trying to get tight jar lids loose and while you might have managed to strain your temper, I bet you never injured your back. According to the Charleston Daily Mail, the lady sued and was awarded a mind-blowing $2,699,000 in punitive damages, $130,066 in compensation, and $179,000 for her emotional distress. Even though one judge in the State Supreme Court called this an "outrageous sum," his was the only dissenting opinion and she got the money. Whether this decision caused a spate of pickle-buying in West Virginia, or further afield, is not recorded.

It happened in a flash

Marlene Seelbinder decided to celebrate the first anniversary of her marriage with a trip to New Smyrna Beach, Florida. While she and her husband were there, a storm blew up and Mrs. Seelbinder was struck by lightning and seriously injured. She maintained that the lifeguards knew the storm was coming but, though they gathered up their own equipment, they gave no warning to members of the public. Apparently, there is a standard policy in place for dealing with storms. If the storm comes within three miles, the beach has to be evacuated. The lifeguards' training manual specifies exactly what steps they should take.

Mrs. Seelbinder stated that the lifeguards knew about the storm 30 minutes before it arrived but failed to give any warning. But counsel for the county, James Smith, countered that before the lightning strike, clouds formed and rain fell. He claimed that the Seelbinders had just as much knowledge of the storm as the lifeguards did. In any case, it is the duty of the lifeguards to alert people to "hidden" dangers and you can hardly call a thunder storm hidden. Mrs. Seelbinder said her health had been wrecked by the incident and she claimed an unspecified amount to cover her enormous medical bills.

Is my butt too big?

A former exotic dancer living in New York decided to have the shape of her butt improved with a little plastic surgery. What she had not expected was that her surgeon would use silicone breast implants to do the job.

When she found out she was not best pleased. In fact, she is quoted as saying, "I looked like I had two [breasts] on my butt." Her surgeon claimed that he did everything right but, even so, a jury awarded her $30,000 to compensate for the "anguish" she had suffered.

It's snow joke

Frederick Puglisi was celebrating New Year in New Jersey. He must have been having a good time because when he walked out into the cold night air, he passed out and collapsed onto a snow bank. He was there for nine hours before being rescued, suffering from frostbite and the effects of exposure. He was lucky not to have died of hypothermia. Apparently, at some stage someone called the emergency services but, for whatever reason, the police failed to take the necessary action. It was alleged that they didn't take down sufficient details from the person who called and, when they visited the scene, they made only a perfunctory search before leaving. Mr. Puglisi's lawyer argued that he was only 15 per cent responsible for what had happened to him and the police were 85 per cent responsible. The jury agreed and awarded him damages of $850,000.

Jackass!

According to CNN.com, a man from Montana is suing the media company Viacom because the MTV show Jackass has plagiarized his name, infringed a trademark and the copyright to his name, and defamed his character. The problem is that the man's name is Jack Ass. No, he wasn't born with the name but he did change it legally in 1977 from Bob Craft. Why did he want such an odd name? He claims it was to raise awareness of the dangers of drunk driving.

If you've never watched Jackass, it shows people performing ridiculous and frequently very dangerous stunts. It was so popular that, in 2002, it was made into a movie.

Mr. Ass claims that Viacom "is liable for injury to my reputation that I have built and defamation of my character which I have worked so hard to create." He's seeking $10 million in damages.

Judgment suspended

When James Roy Cowan Jr. was admitted to the San Antonio State Hospital, he was in a bad state. So bad, in fact, that he decided to commit suicide by hanging himself with his suspenders. His family wanted to sue the hospital for not preventing his suicide, but there was a problem. In Texas, you aren't allowed to sue state entities. They looked for a loophole and found one—you can sue if the state injures someone by using "tangible personal property." So, the argument was that the hospital had misused Mr. Cowan's suspenders by allowing him to keep them to kill himself. Nice try, but the courts were not impressed.

Last straw

Many people, especially those outside the U.S., think that frivolous lawsuits are funny. The stories get told and retold, always with the subtext, "Look what those crazy Americans have done now!" It is only after looking closer at the issue that you begin to see that these endless frivolous lawsuits are not funny at all. They waste public funds, often destroy harmless law-abiding people, and bring the law and lawyers into disrepute.

Take, for example, the case of a woman in Mississippi who discovered that there was a class action lawsuit against a drug called Propulsid. The woman had not suffered any harm from Propulsid but thought that by getting in on the lawsuit, she might make some money. Her doctor was so distressed at being the target of yet another litigious patient who had suffered no real ill effects, that he moved to another state. His wife—also a doctor—went with him and therefore the area was deprived of the services of two doctors because of one too many people's greed.

Let's all do the skank!

Would you be offended if someone called you a skank? This is the question raised by a lawsuit brought against a rock radio station called Alice 97.3 FM. A woman had taken part in a TV show called Who Wants to Marry a Multimillionaire? She lost, but that was the least of her troubles. She then heard her performance discussed on the Sarah and Vinnie Show where she was referred to as a "chicken butt," a "local loser," and "a big skank." The woman was not actually named but, even so, she felt humiliated and so she sued the owners of the radio station, a company called Infinity.

The court was unsympathetic and decided that the words used were no more than a childish taunt. The judge also pointed out that by choosing to take part in the show, the woman had voluntarily invited public scrutiny and ridicule. Finally, he pointed out that "skank" is not a real word and nobody knows what it means. The lawsuit was thrown out.

The woman's attorney was quick to comment that the court was clearly out of touch and that the listeners would certainly have understood the word "skank" all too well. Looking it up on the internet proves an interesting experience. The first meaning given is: "A rhythmic dance performed to reggae or ska music, characterized by bending forward, raising the knees, and extending the hands." This seems harmless, though quite why you would want to call someone a dance was not clear. On reading further, however, you get to a more relevant definition: "one who is disgustingly foul or filthy and often considered sexually promiscuous. Used especially of a woman or girl." Ah, now that would be enough to make anyone mad. An appeal could well be looming.

Model behavior

Konrad Mader, a two-year-old model and actor from Greenwich, Connecticut, was playing happily when he ran toward a tree-house and fell, hitting his head on a railing. The toddler cut his head and needed several stitches. His mother decided to sue the city of Stamford, seeking compensation for medical bills, pain, and suffering. Not content with that, she also demanded a payment for "lost wage amount due to his inability to audition or take modeling or commercial jobs while his head heals." His mother contended that the green railing blended in with foliage around the playground and was therefore hard to see. Had the city done its job properly, it would have had the railings painted in a bright color that made them stand out.

Naughty but not nice

A Canadian man was taking the opportunity to spend a little R&R time in a Vancouver strip club when one of the girls kicked him in the face, presumably by accident. The victim was not amused and sued the club for damages on the grounds of the stripper's "reckless" behavior.

Needle nonsense

The law is so keen to award damages to people who sue that juries can ignore even the most persuasive evidence. For example, a man from South Portland in Maine sued the anesthetist who had attended him during a diagnostic exam some years previously. It was claimed that the needle used during the examination had punctured his bowel and had then proceeded to cause an infection of E. coli in his spine. As a result he suffered from serious back trouble that had forced him to give up work. The interesting bit is this: in Maine they have a rule that any claim for malpractice must be reviewed by a panel of neutral medical experts and lawyers. This had been done and the panel decided unanimously that the man's condition was not the result of the diagnostic exam. So what do you think? Did the jury throw then case out? No way! They awarded the man damages of $3 million.

No April fooling

If you imagine that Americans are happy with their compensation culture, you could not be more wrong. Many people despair at the way the country's legal system is being overrun with loony lawsuits. The American Tort Reform

Association is a body that campaigns against abuse of the legal process in pursuit of frivolous claims. To mark April Fool's Day, they issued a list of cases that seem crazy but, they assure us, are all genuine:

- In Tennessee, a woman sued McDonald's when a hot pickle got dislodged from her burger and allegedly caused permanent scarring on her chin. Her husband is also seeking damages on the grounds that he "has been deprived of the services and consortium of his wife."

- A woman in Illinois also sued McDonald's, Wal-Mart, a cup manufacturer, and her own mother when a cup of hot McDonald's coffee scalded her ankle after it fell out of the Wal-Mart cup holder in her mother's car.

- A prisoner in Texas sued Penthouse magazine on the grounds that he was "very mentally hurt and angered" when a pictorial of Paula Jones was not revealing enough.

- Meanwhile, a prisoner serving time for the armed robbery of a Taco Bell restaurant has grand plans. Not only does he want to be recognized as the Messiah, but he also demands a presidential pardon and the freedom to come and go as he pleases from the Michigan prison where he has been incarcerated for the past 20 years. He claims, because he's God, he owns everything on earth and therefore could not be guilty of robbery.

Not remotely funny

Some people feel that the greatest invention of our time is the remote control. What bliss it is to be able to change the TV channel without leaving the comfort of your chair! As time goes by, the desire for more and more remote controls keeps growing. Some of us have even come to rely on a little gizmo that you attach to your car keys so that you can locate them simply by whistling.

Another ingenious device is called the Clapper—a cunning little gadget that turns the lights on and off without you having to wrestle with those inconvenient light switches. However, one customer was less than happy with her Clapper because she found that she had to clap too hard to make it work. So now she's suing the makers.

On track for a fortune

Most of us have had a few drinks too many, at one time or another, and sometimes you end up regretting it. What exactly did you say to the boss at the office party? How did you get home last night? Well, count yourself lucky that you are not in the shoes of Pedro Duran of Pensacola in Florida. He spent a night out with his friends and got very drunk indeed. In fact he was so far gone that he ended up staggering home on his own late at night. Unfortunately for him, he passed out on a railroad track and he lay there completely insensible until a train came by and lopped off his arm. You know what comes next, of course. Yes, you're right—he sued the railroad. Naturally he won and was awarded $900,000 compensation.

Pug ugly

A jury awarded $5.5 million to the family of a woman who was driven to suicide by what she claimed was harassment and discrimination by her bosses and underlings at the Postal

Service. Judith Coflin's family accused her coworkers of calling her "ugly as a dog," circulating a caricature of her, and leaving a suggestive poem for her at her job at a processing center. They accused her coworkers of intentionally botching jobs or missing deadlines to sabotage her career because she was a woman. Ms. Coflin, a diabetic, overdosed on insulin in 1995, leaving a suicide note blaming the Postal Service. The jury awarded her family $500,000 in compensatory damages and $5 million in punitive damages.

Rave review

Have you seen Sony Pictures' A Knight's Tale? Why? Did it get a good review? You may be interested to know that the company recently admitted to inventing a film reviewer and fabricating quotes. Now guess what? A personal injury lawyer, Mr. Blumenthal, has brought a class action against the company. The case is being brought on behalf of Omar Rezec and Ann Belknap for all the moviegoers who were beguiled into seeing the movie by quotes such as the one that stated the film's lead actor is, "this year's hottest new star." Mr. Blumenthal is quoted as saying that the purpose of his action was not to compensate moviegoers but to punish Sony for deceit.

Shocking events

A bar owner called Jessie Ingram was feeling a tad frustrated because, within a month, his bar had been broken into three times. Jessie had a bright idea. He installed a booby trap that connected his windows to the electricity supply so that anyone tampering with them would be done to a crisp before you could say "barbecue." Realizing that this move might be unpopular with the criminal fraternity, he posted notices around the building warning potential burglars of the damage to their health if they messed with the windows. For a few days all was well, but then Larry Harris, who was later found to be under the influence of booze and cocaine, decided to try his luck. Jessie's booby trap worked just fine and very soon the burglar was cooked to perfection. Apparently, in the state of Illinois you are allowed to use deadly force to protect your property, so the cops were not at all annoyed at Jessie's tactics.

However, the burglar's family decided to sue. Their lawyer claimed that no one could be really sure what Larry Harris had been up to that night and he ought to get the benefit of the doubt. This case was not settled quickly. In fact, it took so long that Jessie died. So that was the end, right? Nope. The suit continued against Jessie's family and eventually a jury awarded the Harris family $150,000. On mature reflection, they considered that Larry Harris was half responsible for his own demise so they cut the payout down to $75,000. The injustice of making people who were not directly involved in the case pay compensation to other people not involved seems to have escaped the jury's notice.

Slip sliding away

This case involves the "Slip'N Slide," a garden toy that consists of a plastic sheet which you inflate with air. You then wet the outside and, hey presto, you have something you can slide about on. The trouble started when a movie company decided to include a scene involving the "Slip'N Slide" in a film called Dickie Roberts: Former Child Star. Apparently the scene involved the actor David Spade going into a mammoth skid and eventually coming to a sudden, and seemingly painful, halt.

The makers of the toy are a company called Wham-O and they wanted the film banned as it contained no warning that Mr. Spade's actions were possibly hazardous and should not be attempted at home. They were concerned that the actor didn't use the slide properly. He did not inflate it, he did not wet the outside, but then he rubbed it with oil. As a result, he crashed into a fence. This scene was something of a highlight of the film and was used in much of the advertising. Wham-O contended that their trademark had been violated because the slide had been used without their permission. They were also concerned that use of the slide is supposed to be for children of ages five to 12, who are less than five feet tall, and weigh less than 110 pounds. Wham-O were concerned that adults might try to imitate Mr. Spade and, in case of injury, might try to sue the makers. It seems that a precursor of the current "Slip'N Slide" had to be withdrawn from sale after a number of adults managed to injure themselves on it. The new product had been improved to make the chance of injury less likely.

Substandard stripper

You wouldn't think that a stripper would have serious problems with customer satisfaction, would you? You get up on stage, move to the music, and take your clothes off. How hard can it be? Well, a 28-year-old male stripper found out to his cost that the price of failure in his profession can be unexpectedly high.

He was engaged to appear at a hen (or bachelorette) party. He didn't get off to a good start because not only did he arrive late but he was not the stripper the party-goers had been expecting, he was a substitute. He didn't exactly make up the lost ground when he failed to pay enough attention to the bride-to-be and then tried to bring his act to a close much sooner than expected. It was at this point that the bride's mother flipped and attacked him. Apparently, he suffered head injuries, scratches, and bruises. He was also hit over the head with a bottle. The police intervened and a court ordered the mother to pay $2,500 in compensation. Now, there is one aspect of this case that no one else seems to have considered. If the lady who proved so handy with a bottle was to be your mother-in-law, wouldn't you feel that perhaps a sharp exit might be in order?

Subway suicide

Just when you think that crazy lawsuits can't get any crazier they go and prove you wrong. For example, when someone reaches a state of desperation so great that they decide to commit suicide, you might be forgiven for thinking that they intend to injure themselves in some way. Call me old fashioned but I never heard of a suicide victim who remained in perfect health after the attempt because that would rather defeat the object, wouldn't it? However, according to the New York Times, a woman who jumped in front of a subway train intending to commit suicide was injured but not killed. So what did she do? Try again? No, she decided to sue and what's more she won. She was awarded damages of $14.1 million.

Suing for Columbine

There can't be many people inside or outside the U.S. who have not heard of the Columbine High School killings. Michael Moore's film Bowling For Columbine is even on the syllabus in some U.K. schools. What you may not have heard is that the parents of Dylan Kelbold, one of the teen killers, have decided to sue Jefferson County sheriff's department and the school district. They contend that they should have had warning of their son's outbursts on the internet and of his friend's tendency to violence. Had they been given fair warning, they would have kept the two boys apart and the murderous escapade would not have got off the ground.

Of course, they might have picked up just the teeniest hint that all was not well if they had found that his room was stuffed with shotguns and pipe bombs.

Tooth trial

According to the Chicago Tribune, a man filed a class action against the American Dental Association and a number of toothbrush manufacturers on the grounds that toothbrushes had caused a disease called "toothbrush abrasion." The plaintiff asserted that it was the responsibility of the toothbrush manufacturers to put notices on their products warning of the dangers of injury while practicing dental hygiene. This lawsuit must send shivers running down the spine of every mother in the U.S. After all, who was it that advised their kids to brush their teeth? Don't you just feel another lawsuit coming on?

Trucker's tribulation

When a trucker's front tire blew, he wound up in a ditch badly injured. In fact, his injuries were so serious that he had to have both legs amputated. He sued and his lawyers maintained that the design of the tire was faulty. They claimed that water had been able to corrode the tire's steal belts. Not surprisingly, the tire company's lawyer disagreed. He claimed that the corrosion was caused by the action of fertilizer from the truck's load on the tire. The court found in favor of the trucker and awarded him damages of $30 million to be paid by the tire manufacturer.

T-shirt trauma

It was the custom at NBC's Tonight Show, hosted by Jay Leno, to propel souvenir T-shirts into the audience. They used some kind of compressed air device to launch the T-shirts and, according to some sources, the clothing traveled at quite a lick before it reached the lucky recipients. None of this impressed audience member Stewart Gregory who claimed that he was struck forcefully in the face by one of the shirts. He is seeking damages of over $47,500 for unspecified injuries, plus the "pain and suffering, disability, lost wages, emotional distress, humiliation, and embarrassment" he endured.

Turbulent times

Air turbulence is one of the hazards of any flight. It can be as alarming as a white-knuckle ride at a fair ground but the good news is that it's not often dangerous. A few minutes bucking and diving before peace is restored. However, 13 passengers on an American Airlines flight decided to sue. They might have reflected that turbulence is a perfectly natural phenomenon that cannot be predicted or prevented by the airline. They might also have thanked their lucky stars that the pilot brought them through in one piece. But the opportunity to get their hands on some compensation proved too much of a temptation. They had suffered no physical injuries but claimed to have suffered psychological trauma. They claimed $2.25 million and they won! The whole turbulence episode lasted about five minutes so that works out at $7,500 per second. Nice work if you can get it.

Toddler's untimely trip

This is one of those lawsuits that is often dismissed as an urban myth but is just as zealously defended by others as being entirely true. You can make up your own mind. It is said that when Kathleen Robertson of Austin, Texas, went furniture shopping, she had the misfortune to trip over a runaway toddler and break her ankle. She sued and a jury awarded her $780,000 in compensation, a decision that outraged the owners of the store. Why? Because the ill-behaved infant was her own son.

Warning—hypocrite at work

This case starts out being just like many others claims for personal injury. A Republican Senator called Ron Wieck filed a lawsuit against a dog owner whose pet bit the senator while he was out campaigning. As always in these cases, the senator is claiming punitive damages, payment for past and future medical bills, loss of clothing damaged in the alleged attack, and for pain and suffering, including anxiety and humiliation. So far so normal. But there is a twist. You see, Senator Wieck was a fervent supporter of House File 692. "What's that?" you ask. It's a legal measure that, if passed, would make it all but impossible for Iowans to get punitive damages if they are seriously injured by the gross negligence of others. The measure was vetoed by Governor Vilsack and the Republicans were in the process of taking legal action. Naturally, Senator Wieck's political enemies were quick to point out the blatant hypocrisy of his actions.

Watch your step, Floyd!

When Floyd Schuler arrived at Southwest Florida International Airport, he'd had a good time on the flight. In fact, he'd had a bit too much of a good time as he'd enjoyed a drink or several on the way. It therefore came as no surprise that he fell down the escalator. He promptly brought a lawsuit seeking $2 million in compensation. So far there is nothing too surprising about this story but what happened next is decidedly odd. Almost as soon as the suit had been filed, it was dropped. Schuler was quoted as saying, "It was never my attempt to take on the airline industry. I apologize for any inconvenience this has caused U.S.

Airways." Hmmm. Filing a lawsuit is not the sort of thing you do on a whim or by accident. Quite what made Floyd change his mind is, and probably will remain, a mystery.

Dirty deluge

When Nancy Todor booked a pleasure cruise for her 43rd birthday party, she no doubt thought that she and her guests were in for a pleasant time and she was right. All her friends aboard the First Lady were having a great time. Until, that is, they passed under the Kinzie Street Bridge. It was here that they were subjected to a two-minute deluge of what can be politely described as liquid human waste (though no doubt Nancy and her friends had other words for it). Think about it. Two minutes may not sound long but if you look at your watch and imagine being showered with liquid poop then you can imagine that it must have felt like an eternity.

The alleged cause of the trouble was a bus owned by the Dave Matthews Band and driven by Stefan Wohl. It is suggested that Mr. Wohl took advantage of the band's absence to get a few chores done—one of them being to empty the bus's 100 gallon sewage tank. Nancy's lawsuit claims that she became "physically ill and extremely nauseous" when hit by the flying poop. She also claims that the, "The liquid human waste went into the passengers' eyes, mouths, hair, and on to clothing and personal belongings—many of which were soaked." In many of the personal injury cases we've reported, it's seemed as if the plaintiff was making a lot of fuss over nothing, but this time it is impossible not to sympathize.

So far, no criminal charge has been brought against the band, though Mr. Wohl has been suspended from duty while a full investigation is carried out. The irony of the whole situation is that the band is known for its eco-friendly stance. They are so green that Ben and Jerry's have named an ice-cream flavor for them. The band has already tried to make amends by donating $200,000 to Chicago's river restoration projects. It is said that Nancy wants them to play a free gig for all those who were on the boat. It's just as well that she seems to be a fan.

Sued by a skater

Two skaters, one a woman and the other a 12-year-old girl, were enjoying themselves on an ice rink in Berkley, Michigan, when they collided. The woman filed suit, claiming that the girl had run into her, knocking her to the ground. As a result of the fall, she sustained a knee injury. When the case came to trial, the woman's claim was rejected because there was no evidence that the girl had behaved recklessly. It was decided that skating has some obvious dangers, and that those who take part accept a level of risk. Then a panel at the Court of Appeals reversed the decision by the lower court and sent the case for trial. Eventually the matter was settled by the Supreme Court which agreed that skating is a risky business and that it is inevitable that there will be accidents and injuries.

Swinging in safety

The manufacturers of a children's swing were sued because a six-year-old fell off while playing in a public park. It was alleged that the design of the swing was faulty and that the seat was loose and wobbled. The kid's claim came to nothing though because the manufacturer showed that the swing was over 20 years old and had been modified in a way that made it dangerous (lock washers intended to keep the seat stable had been removed).

Rear-ended

A Detroit woman was on a bus when a van rear-ended it. She sued on the grounds that she had been injured as a result of the impact. However, the damage to the bus was only slight (just a cracked tail light and a split hose). The driver maintained that at the time of the impact, he had the air brakes on and people who were boarding the bus were not troubled by the accident. The woman lost her case.

Candle scandal

A woman from Grand Have, Michigan, was cleaning her employer's condominium when she came across what she thought was a decorative candle. She decided to take it with her when she went to dinner with some friends and she lit it in the restaurant. What she didn't realize was that the "candle" was a particularly powerful fire cracker. It exploded inflicting serious injuries on her. She sued her employers for leaving the fire cracker lying about without any warning notice attached. The employers said that someone had left the firecracker behind after a party and that they had stored it safely in a cupboard where children couldn't find it.

Wheelie painful

A woman hospital worker was being pushed in a wheelchair. When she came to an entrance ramp, she ignored the purpose-built walkway which was intended for people in wheelchairs. Instead, she tried to go through the parking gate where she was struck on the head. She decided to sue the manufacturers of the gate on the grounds that the blow had caused her injuries to her head, shoulder, and neck. The jury was not impressed and the case was thrown out.

Snow joke

A couple of dogs were allowed out for a run by their owner when they spotted something interesting and gave chase. They raced across a neighboring property and their owner ran after them. In his rush to recapture the dogs he stepped in a snow-covered hole left by a fence post. His foot got caught in the hole and the man suffered injuries as a result. He tried to sue the neighbor for negligence but had no luck. Both the lower and the appeals courts agreed that he was trespassing and therefore the neighbor had no duty to protect trespassers from falling into holes on his property.

Vicious vending

Bronx kids have a reputation for being tough but that didn't help 17-year-old Albert Salcedo. He was in the lunchroom of Theodore Roosevelt High School when he put some money in a Snapple vending machine. The machine ate his dollar but gave nothing back so Albert shook it. He insisted that he only handled the machine "very gently" but whatever he did, it was too much. Albert claimed that the machine must have been top heavy because it fell on him and he suffered a broken foot and ankle. He is now suing the city for $5 million.

The unkindest cut

A woman was chopping vegetables when she had to answer a call of nature. Being in a hurry, she threw the knife down and, by chance, it landed with the blade uppermost. While she was away, a thief crept across the roof and tried to enter the kitchen via a skylight. He lost his grip and, of course, landed on the knife which caused a very nasty wound. Naturally he's suing.

Sued Samaritan

Cobb's Inn and one of its waiters, Paul Kane, are being sued because Paul did a customer a good deed. Jefferson Ketcham was drunk and Paul offered him a lift home. When he got out of the car, he was so out of it that he tripped, hit his head, and died. The family are suing on the grounds that Paul should have walked Ketcham all the way to the door.

Drink disaster

Amber Carson of Lancaster, Pennsylvania, was on a date with her boyfriend when, during their meal at a local restaurant, they got into an argument. Amber's boyfriend got so steamed up that she decided to cool him down a little and threw her drink over him. She then got up and was presumably about to walk out, when she slipped on the wet patch she had just created. She fell heavily, breaking her coccyx. She sued the restaurant and was awarded $113,500.

Brick blows

A building worker in England was leaning out from the scaffolding to shout instructions to a colleague down below when a brick fell from a higher floor and struck him on the head.

Fortunately, he was wearing his hard hat and, though it got knocked off by the force of the blow, it saved him from serious injury. Unfortunately, another brick fell a couple of seconds later and struck him a savage blow. He suffered severe head injuries and sued his employer for negligence.

Babysitting blues

Like many young women Erica Bailey, 21, earned extra money by doing some babysitting. One of the kids hit her in the throat and, allegedly, changed her voice permanently, making it sound husky. She is suing for £1.5 million ($2.8 million) but, if she doesn't get it, a career as a blues singer beckons.

Chapter Three:
A Life of Crime

Writ for writer

Writers are always concerned about the possibility of being sued for libel but this case boggles the mind. A serial killer from Orange County, California, had been caught, convicted, and was on death row awaiting execution. When he saw a book that detailed his crimes, he tried to sue the author for $100 million. The convict claimed that he was innocent of the 16 murders with which he had been charged and therefore the book had "defamed his good name." He also maintained that the book would cause him to be, "shunned by society and unable to find decent employment." To the credit of the authorities, it took under a minute to dismiss his case, but even so the writer's publisher had to foot a bill of $30,000 in legal fees.

A fast exit

Regular viewers of the British version of the quiz show Who Wants to be a Millionaire were puzzled when Major Charles Ingram won the jackpot prize but the TV company refused to pay out. Some of the other contestants were clearly furious and the usual atmosphere of euphoria that usually accompanied a big win was absent. It was all explained when, shortly after the show, it was revealed that Ingram, his wife, and a friend called Tecwen Whittock had been accused of cheating and the police were asked to investigate a possible fraud. It emerged that Whittock had been guiding Ingram to the correct answers by a series of coded coughs. The three of them were lucky to get away without being imprisoned.

This bizarre case did not end with the trial, however. There was an appeal which failed. Also, the low-cost airline EasyJet ran an ad in the press using pictures of Ingram and his wife. The strapline read "Need a cheap getaway? (No major fraud required)." The Ingrams complained to the Advertising Standards Authority which heard their case and dismissed it.

Bloody nonsense

One of the most litigious sectors of the population is the criminal element. It is amazing how people who are locked up can use their excessive amounts of spare time to conduct unlikely lawsuits. This one is a lulu. In 2000, when Robert Paul Rice was banged up for 1–15 years for various felonies, he gave his religion as Catholic. However, his incarceration obviously gave him the leisure to reconsider his religious opinions and, after what was no doubt a long inner struggle, he converted. I bet you can't guess what he decided to be. A Buddhist? A Jew? Maybe a Seventh Day Adventist? Oh no, nothing as simple as that. He decided that he was now a Druidic Vampire. Even in Wales where they still know what Druids are all about, you can be sure that no one has heard of a Druidic Vampire. This didn't concern Mr. Rice one bit. He claimed that he was being denied the opportunity to practice his religion. What he needed was sexual relations with a "vampress" and the opportunity to consume blood as a regular part of his diet. Did he succeed? No way. A nice try, but in the end the authorities dismissed his complaint.

Brain damage

A woman whose husband was murdered by her son had more than the usual reasons to be upset. She maintains that when the coroner came to collect the body, he didn't do a good job. In fact, he left the victim's brain behind because it had fallen on the floor where he failed to notice it. Also it seems as though the brain was subsequently thrown out and lost. The woman is not only mad her husband will go to meet his maker minus one of his vital organs, she also contends that the brain might have been vital evidence that could have had an effect on her son's trial for murder.

Convict claims

Here's another lawsuit filed by a prisoner. One of the problems of being in prison must be sheer boredom: there's all that time to fill in and not much to do. Another problem is lack of money. Who wants to come out of jail and be poor? One way to solve both problems is to sue the authorities. This gives the inmates something to do and, with luck, provide them with a nice little nest egg when they are freed. An inmate in California took this idea to extremes when he sued the state because he maintained that the chili he was served was too hot.

D.I.Y.

To understand this case, you need to cultivate an "Alice in Wonderland" mentality. There have been other cases of convicts trying to bring lawsuits but this one is in a league of its own. A prisoner decided to file a lawsuit against himself. He was claiming $5 million in damages because, he reasoned, he had violated his own civil rights by getting caught. Now comes the twist: he wanted the state to pay the money because he was in prison and therefore had no income. He is reported as saying: "I want to pay myself $5 million dollars, but ask the state to pay it on my behalf since I can't work and am a ward of the state." The case was dismissed as being frivolous.

Embezzled bucks

People are prone to complaining that banks are so keen to hold onto as much money as possible that sometimes they aren't too fussed about where all the loot comes from. Some banks, however, do have high ethical standards and it was one of these companies that got into trouble. Having realized that it was holding millions of embezzled dollars, the bank found out who was legally entitled to the money and then paid it all back. However, someone operating as an accomplice of the embezzler sued the bank and sought damages of $20 million. The case was thrown out by the court but only after the bank had been forced to run up a bill of $20,000 in lawyers' fees.

Free fall

This one is not yet a lawsuit but, given what we know about the way prison inmates love nothing better than suing the authorities, it can only be a matter of time before there is a claim for damages.

Ben N. Rogozensky is our unlucky convict. He was taken from prison in Decatur, Georgia, to a court hearing. He wanted to consult his lawyer and was allowed to do so in the empty jury room. Then he asked to go to the bathroom and, while he was in there, he accessed the crawl space above the ceiling and made a bid for freedom.

Now Ben was clearly not the most nimble of men because he soon managed to fall through the ceiling and landed, as ill luck would have it, in the judge's office. He was re-captured without a struggle. The point is this: just how long will it take Ben to realize that far from being a recaptured felon, he is in fact a wronged plaintiff who should be compensated for his injuries caused by the recklessness and negligence of the authorities? Did they attempt to persuade him not to escape? Did they post warnings in the crawl space about what might happen to people who crawled across ceilings? Exactly. This looks like an open and shut case and if he can't squeeze $1 million out of it then he should be ashamed of himself!

Gun crime

It would take a book many times the size of this one to discuss thoroughly America's enduring love affair with guns, but one case did catch my eye. It seems that one result of the welter of legal action following the 2002 Washington sniper shootings is that the makers of the Bushmaster rifle (the type with which most of the shootings were carried out) have agreed to pay $550,000 in compensation to the victims' families. The shop from which the gun was stolen (Bull's Eye Shooter Supply in Tacoma, Washington) is paying $2 million. Now, you can see how sloppy security that allows lethal weapons to be stolen deserves to be penalized. But why would you sue a gunsmith for making a gun? This is a perfectly lawful activity and, in the U.S. where owning guns is a practice that is approved by many, it is hardly surprising that someone is going to manufacture them. You can, if so minded, carry out violent attacks with all sorts of legally-owned objects (cars, knives, even knitting needles), but should the manufacturer always be responsible for the uses to which the product is put? It seems illogical.

Hot pants

Just sometimes, despite all the lawyers can do to prevent it, justice actually prevails. In this case, a convicted robber was let out on parole and decided to return to his former profession. He robbed a branch of California Savings and Loan. He seized the money roll and stuffed it into the front pocket of his pants. Now here comes the good bit. Within the money roll was something called a Security Pac. It's a neat little device designed to deter thieves. When disturbed, it releases tear gas and sprays red dye. It also, apparently, gets very hot because our robber found himself in A&E being treated for serious burns to his tender regions. He has tried to sue the bank, the makers of Security Pac, the city, the police, and the hospital. The case is ongoing.

Killed on the job

On a bright mid-summer's day, Jonathon Russell, of Jefferson City, Missouri, had planned a busy day at work. He took his gun with him and opened fire on his colleagues. Not satisfied with that, he then drove down to the local police station and opened fire on the police as well. Bad move, Jonathon! The police shot back at him and eventually he decided it would be best to turn the gun on himself. So where does the lawsuit come in to all this? His mother claimed that his death was work related. She tried to bring a case in which she described what had happened as, "Death by gunfire while on company clock [time]." Nice try, mom, but it didn't work.

Kismet

You may have forgotten the name Mehmet Ali Agca, but you will remember him when I tell you that he is the guy who shot the Pope. While languishing in jail, he heard something that strangely interested him. You may or may not know but each Pope receives the third secret of Fatima. Quite what that is we can't tell you—if you really want to know, you have to become Pope. However, Pope John Paul II revealed that the secret helped him to see that he would be the victim of an assassination attempt. The would-be assassin has now made a plea for clemency on the grounds that his crime was preordained and therefore no fault of his. Experts on both criminal and canon law don't fancy his chances of success, but you have to give him an A for effort.

Knave or fool?

A good barrister (or trial lawyer) is always something of an actor. He knows that the jury can be swayed as much by his brilliant oratory, as by the facts of the case. Indeed, sometimes they will happily fly in the face of facts and vote for the barrister who demonstrates the most skill in presenting his case. Sir Henry Curtis-Bennett was just such a man. In one of his most famous cases, the argument came down to this: the defendant was either a crook or a fool. Sir Henry liked to give juries a brilliant parting shot just before they retired to consider their verdict. His closing remark was, "You may think my client a fool. I tell you myself he is a fool. But you can't convict on that or the courts would be full!"

Miami vice?

A guy was staying at a Miami hotel when he got shot. His family decided to sue the hotel chain for $1.7 million on the grounds that it did not do enough to protect its guests' lives. Now, if you think about the sheer size and complexity of most hotels, you'll see immediately that this is plain stupid. The whole point of a hotel is that people are coming and going at all hours. You can't strip search every one of them or you'd have no guests. But in this case, there is a twist in the tale. It turns out that the dead guy was involved in a drug transaction that went wrong. OK, so now we know that the people involved were criminals engaged in an illegal act. So, of course, there could be no question of compensation now, could there? Oh yes, the family won.

Nutrition notes

Even criminals have their rights and, as we have seen, they are not slow to claim them by using the courts where necessary. One convict serving time in California was worried that when he bought chips from the jail's canteen, the packet did not have nutritional information printed on it. How is a guy going to make an informed choice about his health in these circumstances? Lacking the necessary information, he claimed that he had "suffered health problems directly related to not being aware of the nutrition information." The result of his lawsuit is awaited with interest.

The importance of being Frank

Frank G. Spisak has a problem. Not only has he been locked up in an Ohio prison for 17 years, but the authorities refuse to call him by his chosen name. You see, Frank longs to be known as Francis Anne. He now wants compensation for the fact that throughout his sentence, he has been harassed because prison officials have insisted on keeping him in an all male environment. The authorities are not sympathetic—as far as they are concerned, he's a man and he'll stay a man until he's released. Unless, of course, some court decides differently.

Prison porn

Things were not going well for Gary Bradford Cone. First of all, he got thrown into a Tennessee jail. Then, to add to his discomfort, the state enacted a new law prohibiting the use of pornography. Cone decided to sue because he maintained that they had taken away his "right" to enjoy pornography. No doubt the porn was useful in keeping his mind off his present problems, because not only is Cone in jail, but he's on death row.

Potato problem

Life was being unkind to Kenneth Williams of San Diego, California. Not only was he awaiting trial for raping an underage girl, but while in prison he was served mashed potatoes containing an unexpected source of protein—a dead fly. He sued the prison authorities for the "mental distress and anguish" he had suffered.

Prison protest

Call me naive but I always thought that the point of prison was for it to be unpleasant. People are sent there as a punishment so it stands to reason that they aren't going to enjoy the same facilities as they would at home. But no, it seems this view is completely out of date. In Massachusetts, the inmates of a county jail sued because they were subjected to cruel and unusual living conditions. They were expected to live in cells that had no sink or W.C., and they had to sleep in bunk beds. As though that were not enough, they were also not provided with a suitable place to take exercise in the winter. Now if you pay your taxes in Massachusetts, you will no doubt be happy to know that you have paid your tax dollars to compensate the convicts for this outrageous state of affairs. The court awarded the prisoners $2 million and every convict got $10 for each day they had been jailed.

Remember my name!

Don't you just hate it when people forget your name? If they keep on doing it, you begin to wonder if there isn't something really Freudian going on. OK, this brings us to Rufus Averhart who decided that the name he'd had from birth was a "slave name" and he wanted a change. He decided, after what can only have been long and careful consideration, to call himself Zolo Agona Azania and in 1991 he adopted the name legally. Now comes the problem: Rufus/Zolo was a prisoner on death row and the staff at the jail just couldn't get their heads around his new name so they kept using the old one. Eventually, he decided to sue for discrimination and religious persecution. By now, you must be well used to the idea of prison inmates brightening the dull days of confinement with a little litigation. However, it turns out that Rufus/Zolo was something of a litigation addict and had over two dozen other law cases on the go. Staff at the jail were resigned to the fact that, unless or until he was executed, they had years more legal fun to look forward to.

Suing for spiders

Prisoners show so much ingenuity in thinking up new lawsuits to help pass the dreary years that you wonder why they never managed to find a really lucrative legal career.

For example, Marcia Wall, who is imprisoned in the Washington State Prison, Davisboro, for burglary and aggravated assault, is suing the authorities on the grounds that the prison is infested with spiders. These aren't the normal run-of-the-mill house spiders either; these little beasts bite. The authorities maintain that they have the prison fumigated on a monthly basis—being assaulted by arachnids is not a part of the punishment and they try to keep it from happening. Ms. Wall's attorney has been sent numerous dead spiders as proof of the size of the problem. The inmates hope that this case will make the authorities do something to get the spider problem under control.

The Queen's memory lapse

The story so far: After Princess Diana's death in a Paris underpass, there was a power struggle among those who wanted to "protect her memory." Paul Burrell, who had been her butler and who she apparently referred to as her "rock," was found to have some of her personal possessions stored in his house. His defense was that the items had been entrusted to him for safe-keeping. The police didn't buy his story and so Burrell was put on trial, accused of stealing the items. It was only just before he was due to take the stand that the Queen had a remarkable flashback—she quite clearly remembered that Burrell had in fact told her that he had taken some of Diana's possessions and was storing them. Naturally, at this point, the prosecution's case collapsed. None of this, of course, had anything at all to do with the fact that Burrell was privy to some very dangerous inside information about the doings of members of the royal family (including a tape in which a former palace servant made accusations about a sexual act he had seen which had involved one of the royals). If ever Mr. Burrell were to choose to tell all he knows, it would make a very interesting story indeed. But somehow it seems likely certain matters will be left unresolved while those affected still live.

Drunk but not detained

A woman got so drunk that she didn't know what she was doing. The next day, however, all she could remember was that she had blundered into a police officer who had failed to arrest her. She was outraged that she had not been taken into protective custody, so she sued. Quite how she remembered which officer it was remains a mystery because at the trial she admitted to being very drunk—too drunk to drive, for example. The case was thrown out by both the lower court and the Appeals Court. It was decided that the officer's duty did not extend to providing protective custody.

Flatulent felon

As we have seen, there is a problem with prisoners who keep suing the authorities on frivolous grounds. In one case, an inmate sued because he claimed that the prison food had caused him to suffer from a flatulence problem. When the Michigan Assistant Attorney General testified before the Michigan Senate Judiciary Committee, he pointed out that such lawsuits were costing the state a fortune. Apparently the bill, paid by state taxpayers, runs to millions of dollars a year.

Cocaine chicks

Whatever you think about lawyers, you can't say they lack chutzpah. In this case, a man called Francisco Armando Rivera ran a cock-fighting den. When it was raided by police, they discovered a gun and 136 pounds of cocaine in a cage that also contained a rooster and two hens. The police arrested Rivera and charged him with possessing the cocaine. However, his lawyer tried to get him off by claiming that the drugs were actually in the possession of the rooster and hens. As he said: "...the law is very clear that whoever is in possession of the drugs is the one who should be accused."

Princess problems

A Saudi princess is suing American Express for $2.2 million because they allowed her spend huge amounts that she could not afford to repay. She maintains that they should have noticed her "irrational" spending and stopped her. Presumably, if they gave the matter any thought at all, they would have reckoned that lavish spending is just a normal day at the office for Saudi royalty.

What they didn't know was that the princess was bogus. Her real name was Antoinette Millard and she was a worker on Wall Street. Far from being born in Saudi Arabia, she was actually a native of Buffalo. She is being tried on charges of fraud.

Toes are a no-no

In The Netherlands, the Dutch Labor Party wants to introduce a law to make unsolicited toe-licking a crime. Apparently, a 35-year-old man with an obsession about women's toes has been making a considerable nuisance of himself for the past three years. There is no problem identifying or apprehending the culprit but, because of the unfortunate way in which the laws are phrased, he has not committed any actual crime, and the victims are unable to sue because what he is doing does not count as an assault. Until such time as a suitable law is passed, all the Dutch ladies can do to avoid his intentions is to keep their shoes on.

Do you want milk with that?

According to the Scottish Daily Record, Colin Hancock, a convicted drug dealer serving time in Perth Prison, Scotland, filed a lawsuit in October, asking for about $55,000 because of an improper rectal exam. The exam was in response to his symptoms of a urine blockage and was given by prison physician. Dr. Alexander MacFarlane, who said he was forced to use, as a lubricant, milk from a bowl of porridge because that was all that was available at the time.

Trouble with the Neighbor

It was reported in northern Italy that a burglar took such a liking to the house of his elderly victim that he moved in. He discovered that the old man who owned the house was too frail to get up the stairs so he decided to take over the upper floor for his own use. He lived very comfortably in the house for some months and even made regular night time forays into the lower floor to steal food and wine. He was eventually caught when a neighbor spotted a light in an upper window and called the cops. The elderly host is now threatening to sue for the rent that he feels he is owed.

Chapter Four:
Business Battles

Video nasty

These days, most of us think nothing of setting the video to record our favorite TV programs for viewing when it suits us best. So you might not know that when video recorders were first introduced in the 1970s, there was a great clamor from the entertainment industry to ban their use for anything but playing pre-recorded tapes. Of course, they were only too happy to be able to sell videos of movies. That was cash straight in their pocket. But any copying that the public wanted to do for themselves was opposed. Lawsuits were filed alleging breach of copyright. What they had not considered was that the early video machines were very expensive and no one would have bought them if all they did was play pre-recorded movies. Fortunately the industry was saved by the courts from its own lunacy. The courts ruled that the public could legally record signals that were broadcast over the airwaves.

Barbie as art

"Don't mess with the mouse," is a popular saying among the U.S. legal profession and refers to the extreme eagerness shown by Disney to sue anyone who they think has infringed their rights. Another useful warning which, as far as I'm aware, is not yet in circulation is, "Don't dis the doll." This refers to the tenacity with which the toymakers Mattel defend the honor of Barbie, one of their best-selling products.

Take Paul Hansen, an artist from San Francisco, who had the idea of creating what he dubbed "Barbie art." He would take ordinary dolls and rework them into humorous versions, such as Trailer Trash Barbie and Exorcist Barbie. His contention was that art is usually not subject to copyright challenges—in other words, if you take an object and alter it substantially then it becomes art. So, even if the original object's copyright belonged to someone else, you now have your own copyright of the artwork. Faced with the legal might of Mattel (who were claiming damages of over a billion dollars!) he very sensibly backed down, and looked for the least expensive way out of the fix. He agreed not to sell any more Barbie art to stores and to confine his activities to art galleries. Mattel weren't satisfied and wanted to go to trial to get a stricter definition of "art gallery." The whole thing dragged on for a year and the judge got so utterly fed up with Mattel that, eventually, he handed down a partial judgment against them on the grounds that they had no sense of humor.

CD tactics

The popularity of swapping music files has caused consternation in the recording industry. Their interests are represented in the U.S. by the Recording Industry Association of America (RIAA) and they have come up with a desperate solution to the problem. They are using their draconian powers to sue anybody found in possession of illicit music files. They have spread their net wide and are taking legal action against everybody from school kids to grannies. They forced a 12-year-old girl to pay $2,000 or face a lawsuit. They tried to prosecute a 66-year-old grandmother until she proved that she did not possess a computer able to make and swap music files. Similar moves are now being considered in other countries. Quite what the recording industry feels it will achieve by alienating the very people who are its customers, is unclear.

Dungeon doll

As previously mentioned, there is nothing as likely to get you into legal hot water than messing with the copyright of Mattel's Barbie doll. An enterprising British doll maker came up with a novel idea—a scantily clad "Dungeon Doll" doll equipped with a rubber bondage dress and helmet. Whatever turns you on... Mattel sued because they claimed that the Barbie lookalike violated their copyright. A judge ruled that the Dungeon Doll was not similar enough to Barbie to amount to a breach of copyright. She said that the new doll was, "quite different from that typically appearing on Mattel's products for children." The judge permitted the action to go forward but Mattel's chances of success seem poor. A BD-SM doll seems unlikely competition for the clean-living all-American Barbie that children all over the world know and love.

Is Barbie a bimbo?

When the Danish techno-pop group Aqua released a song called Barbie Girl, it was just one of those silly summer songs that makes its way into the charts because people find it impossible not keep humming the tune to themselves. Mattel were not amused (again). They saw the song as bringing Barbie's reputation into disrepute. Even a disclaimer on the record that said: "The song Barbie Girl is a social commentary and was not created or approved by the makers of the doll," failed to mollify them.

They disliked the dialogue between Barbie (played by Lene Grawford Nystrom) and her boyfriend Ken (Rene Dif) which they thought contained references to sexual domination and humiliation. Mattel objected to phrases in the song, such as "hanky-panky," "touch me there," and references to the character as a "blonde bimbo girl."

The company disliked the "veiled sexual content" which it thought inappropriate bearing in mind that the doll is intended for girls in the 3–11 age group. They complained particularly about the way that Barbie was portrayed a bimbo. In 2003, Mattel lost its legal battle against MCA records when the US Supreme Court upheld a previous ruling in favor of the record company. They decreed that the song commented humorously on society and its values and was protected by the First Amendments rights to free speech.

Kids' stuff

You'd have to be a member of an enclosed religious order, or perhaps living in Outer Mongolia, not to recognize Tony the Tiger who has been advertising Kellogg's Frosted Flakes ("They're grrrrreat!") for many years. If you think that cartoon characters are just kids' stuff, don't be fooled. There are big bucks at stake in the cartoon business and it is a fine place for launching lawsuits.

In this case Hasbro, the giant toy-making company, took offense because it seems that Tony looks too much like a figure from some memory game that they used to make back in the 1960s. It was eventually decided to settle the affair rather than risk a long and costly battle. Hasbro licensed its Memory trademark to Kelloggs for use in a Finding Nemo game that it was running in conjunction with Disney.

Love thy neighbor?

In 1991, Arnold Abbott started a charity called Love Thy Neighbor in memory of his late wife. The business of the charity is to help the homeless of Broward County, Florida. However, in Detroit there is a jewelry company called Love Your Neighbor belonging to Catherine Sims, who had the foresight to trademark the phrase "love thy neighbor." Ms. Sims decided to sue the charity on the grounds that it was creating confusion that resulted in her company suffering lost sales and profits. Not only does she want damages, but she also wants to stop Mr. Abbott's charity from using its present name. The charity is not a wealthy one, it has a budget of less than $90,000 per annum and is run by a staff of volunteers, so there just isn't the money to spend on litigation. Mr. Abbott is particularly sore that a biblical phrase (taken from Matthew 19:19) should have been allowed to be trademarked.

Making heavy weather of it

Normally we think of filing loony lawsuits as being a very American pastime. But, hey, why shouldn't the Brits have some fun too? The weather forecasting agency in the U.K. is called the Met Office and it owns a registered logo. Apparently the New York Mets baseball team wanted to register their own logo in the U.K. so that they could sell baseball-related goodies on the far side of the pond. This is unlikely ever to become a major source of income because, apart from a few dedicated enthusiasts, the Brits don't play baseball. Even so, the Met

Office claimed that the N.Y.M. logo would be confused with theirs. The matter was taken to the British Trademarks Register where it was decided that any confusion would be most unlikely and therefore the Mets should be allowed to register their trademark in the U.K.

Oodles of Googles

Although the whole world must by now have heard of the search engine Google, you could be excused for not knowing that Googles.com is a children's Web portal. The extra "s" makes all the difference. Googles has now filed complaints against Google because it is breaching copyright laws by offering services aimed at children. Googles invented cute cartoon aliens called the "Googles from Goo" and applied for copyright in 1997. The rights were sold to Stelor Productions in 2002. On the Googles site, kiddies can find email, games, and an online diary. There is also shopping aimed at two- to 10-year-old children.

The thing that most annoys Googles is that Google has now launched a price-matching service called Froogles which might affect Googles marketing of children's toys, clothes, and books. The rivals may see this fight as terribly serious but the rest of us will dissolve in a fit of the giggles.

Psychic but silly

In Aspen, Colorado, a legal wrangle has developed between two psychics. One of them claims that the other has illegally copied her business name—Aspen Psychic. You would imagine that psychics would have an advantage over the rest of us because, presumably, their supernatural powers will let them know what will happen in the future. Indeed, the plaintiff does claim that she knew the lawsuit was coming: "Because I was told through my visions that evil was trying to enter a very sacred place." This might sound impressive if it were not for the fact that the defendant has also used her psychic power to reassure herself that she will win. Let's hope the jury will find the correct verdict written in their tea leaves.

Russian rivals

Two young Russian composers were locked in battle over a piece of music which each claimed had been plagiarized by the other. The court was stumped. How could the truth be discovered? It was decided to summon Alexander Porfir'yevich Borodin as an expert witness.

Borodin was a man of the highest reputation, being not only a distinguished composer but also a professor of chemistry. He listened to both pieces of music in turn and then the judge asked, "Well, Alexander Porfir'yevich, who do you think wrote the original version?" "Without question," replied the great man, "it was my friend Mussorgsky."

Satan's soap

This is a case so long and convoluted that a detailed version of the story would take up a whole book on its own. We'll stick to the short version but, if you have the patience, you can get hold of the court records and read it for yourself.

It starts with the two giant soap companies Amway and Proctor & Gamble (P&G). For many years, there had been odd stories about P&G that suggested the company was in some way linked to Satanism. P&G maintain that Amway were behind the rumors and were fostering them as a means of destroying their rival's reputation. There is almost nothing to substantiate such rumors. It has been said that a P&G executive appeared on a TV chat show (versions differ, it could have been Donahue, The Tonight Show, or David Letterman) and admitted that he was a Satanist. Another rumor says that the chairman of the P&G board sold his soul to the Devil in return for success in the soap selling business.

If all this were not stupid enough, we now come to the P&G logo. It shows an old man with a beard and 13 stars. Quite what it's meant to represent is anyone's guess but those who support the Satanist theory have their own interpretation. Apparently, the old man's hair forms a devil's horn and the curls in his beard make the number 666, the number of the beast. If you join up the 13 stars in just the right way and look at them through a mirror they also make the number of the beast. These are charges that P&G felt had to be answered. The legal battle rumbled on for seven years, until eventually a judge was so fed up with the whole thing that he blew his top. He said: "Although no decision from this court—or any other, we predict— will end the hatred these two corporate giants harbor for each other... we hope that they will consider the impact of their continuing legal battle on the scarce resources of the courts, and decide to concentrate their creative talents on the more traditional method of gaining competitive advantage and declare a ceasefire in the judicial arena."

Crazy Caterpillar

Disney is world famous for its cute cartoon characters and sentimental plot lines. If you heard that they were making a movie in which wild animals protect their habitat from those greedy to exploit it for commercial gain, would you be surprised? No, of course not. That is exactly the sort of feel-good movie that they are known for. However, the folks at Caterpillar, makers of heavy earth-moving equipment, were less than thrilled when they heard about the plot of the movie George of the Jungle 2. They felt that their reputation was in jeopardy because bulldozers were being shown as destroyers of the environment. How long do you think it will be before a lawsuit is filed?

Trespass trouble?

No matter how dumb some lawsuits are, you have to give the plaintiffs credit for originality. A couple in Michigan were annoyed by the dust, noise, and vibrations that reached their property from a nearby business. They claimed that the dust and debris were entering their property without their permission and so they sued for trespass. Initially they had some success but the Court of Appeals overturned a favorable verdict from the lower court. It was decided that dust, noise, and vibrations are all intangibles and cannot be trespassers.

He that steals my good name...

In business, a lot can hang on a name and companies are always on the lookout for people who would try to cash in on a name they don't own. Sometimes, however, things go just a little too far. The Mayo Clinic, for example, sued the makers of a low-calorie mayonnaise called "Mayo." Stupid? Yes, but not unique. The makers of Berreta guns (the ones favored by James Bond before he changed to the more macho Walther P.P.K.), sued General Motors for using the name Beretta on an automobile. The gun makers claimed that this use would "dilute" their brand.

Toy tantrum

Play-Doh has been almost standard issue for a whole generation of kids. But Kenner Parker Toys, the manufacturers, were unhappy when a rival company came up with the Tyco Double Dough Doer. Apparently, the fiendish device allowed the child to push two colors of Play-Doh through the machine. Of course, if anyone got hold of the idea that you can make perfectly good dough from flour, water, salt, and food coloring then Kenner Parker Toys might lose a lot of dough themselves.

A weighty affair

A company called Pillsbury has as its mascot the Doughboy. Over 20 years ago, a rival firm called the Sunshine Biscuit Company invented a character called Drox. It seemed that the two characters could exist amicably side-by-side until Pillsbury noticed that Drox was gaining a few pounds. They reckoned that the new plumper Drox was a cynical attempt to imitate their Doughboy so they sued.

Raisin objections

Kellogg's, whose products have been familiar on breakfast tables throughout the world for many years, decided to sue General Foods for $100 million. Why? Because they objected to ads for Post Raisin Bran. They claimed that Post Natural Raisin Bran could not be natural because it is coated with coconut oil. General Foods had another headache when they were sued by Uncle Ben's because they had claimed that their Minute Rice outperformed Uncle Ben's in something called "the slotted spoon test."

Chapter Five:
On the Job

Tackling Tourette's

Tourette's syndrome is a strange and terrible disability. The sufferer is prone to sudden and violent muscular spasms which cause uncontrollable twitching. Depending on the severity of the case, this can mean anything from minor involuntary muscular movements to full-blown paroxysms in which the victim is completely at the mercy of the twitches for brief, but highly embarrassing, periods. This, however, is not the full extent of the harm Tourette's can do. Sufferers are also subject to what is known as "coprolalia" a fancy name for something really ugly. They have an irresistible and uncontrollable urge to shout obscenities, racial slurs, and other remarks of a thoroughly objectionable nature.

The public at large are not very sympathetic to Tourette's sufferers because most people simply don't understand that the person concerned is a helpless victim of an incurable condition. This brings us to the case of Karl Petzold who worked in a

Farmer Jack supermarket as a bagger. Customers were offended when he shouted obscenities. Blacks and women were especially insulted by the things he called them. The store felt that Karl's outbursts might make them liable to prosecution under legislation designed to deal with what is known as a "customer hostile environment." So they sacked Karl and he sued on the grounds that his disability should not have cost him his job. The last we heard was that the Michigan Court of Appeals was considering this tricky problem.

A rude awakening

John Hauschild was fond of a little nap during the day. In fact, he was so fond of his siesta that the management of the waste water treatment plant in Omaha where he was a foreman decided to keep tabs on him. They rather sneakily installed a tiny camera in his computer and guess what? On every one of the 15 days recorded, he was caught having an illicit nap. Naturally they sacked him and it will come as no surprise that he sued and demanded reinstatement. The grounds for his lawsuit were that the city did not properly disclose the evidence against him and also that he suffered from a sleeping disorder. Though he lost his case before the city's personnel board, he appealed to the court and won. No doubt the court's decision caused some loss of sleep among Hauschild's bosses.

Fundamental error

When you think of Saudi Arabia (which you probably don't very often) you might reflect on its oil reserves, its strict enforcement of Islamic law, and its super-rich royal family. What you don't think about is the sewage problems of its capital city, Jeddah. But you would if you lived there—oh yes.

You see, many years ago it was decided to build an efficient, modern system. The guy who got the contract thought it would be a lot more fun to build himself a nice house in Jeddah and another in San Francisco. Actually the word "nice" scarcely does his houses justice. Let's just that that if he went on MTV's show Cribs you wouldn't be surprised. He is now being sued by Hussein Shobokshi—a building contractor and part-time journalist—because sewage has leaked into the city's groundwater and the drinking water is contaminated. This has led to a great increase in diseases such as hepatitis, not to mention certain cancers. When he investigated further, Shobokshi was advised by foreign experts that the city was sitting on a powder keg. Raw sewage had been pumped into a lake just outside the city. The lake is in a prime site for earthquakes and is lined with nothing but sand. If there were to be an earthquake the entire city would soon be engulfed in a tide of slurry.

Now what intrigues me is this: in a country where you can get your hand chopped off as punishment for a bit of thieving, why can you only be sued for putting the health of the capital at risk? I'm only asking because I would really like to know.

Hell hath no fury...

Getting romantically involved with patients is always a troublesome area for medics. In this case, a woman had been treated by a psychiatrist for eight months. They married a few years later, but, after only five years of marriage, they filed for divorce. At this point, the woman alleged that when they began their relationship she was still receiving treatment. She claimed that her ex-husband had breached the standard of care expected of a psychiatrist and sued him for damages.

I call your name, but you're not there

Lillie Anderson was sick of her job. So sick, in fact, that she went to her supervisor and announced that she had had enough and was going home. The supervisor, who was taken by surprise, merely called out Lillie's name. The company contends that this did not constitute permission to leave work. Lillie, however, felt ill and went home. She thought that telling her supervisor what she intended to do was sufficient warning. The company sacked her because she was judged guilty of willful misconduct. Lillie was denied unemployment compensation. The court found in the company's favor.

Lawyer licked!

It's not often that you hear about lawyers suing and coming unstuck so this case is really one to savor. In 1999, a medical malpractice suit was filed against a gynecological oncologist in Pennsylvania. The lawsuit came two years after the doctor had performed tests on a patient suspected of having cervical cancer. As a result of a biopsy, it was found that the patient did not have cancer. As you might expect, the judge found in favor of the doctor and so the doctor sued the woman's lawyer. The case was eventually settled out of court. Now comes the good bit: the lawyer was forced to make the following public statement: "I did not at any time, either before I filed suit or afterward, obtain an opinion from a qualified medical expert regarding the doctor's treatment. I also understand now... that it hurts to be the target of a lawsuit and its critical allegations even if you know they are without merit."

Lawyer lover

Who loves a lawyer? No, don't laugh, this is a serious question. At least one lady found it in her heart to form a romantic attachment to an attorney. The only problem was that the attorney happened to be the one who had defended her husband on a charge of murder. The husband had been convicted and sent to jail and only found out about his wife's love affair later. The lawyer maintained that the fact that his former client was jailed had nothing to do with the affair, but the court wasn't happy and ordered a re-trial. The lawyer was disbarred for two years.

Legal aid for illegal aliens

You would probably assume that one of the first rules of being an illegal alien would be, "sit tight and keep your mouth shut." You might also assume that when the authorities find illegals working, they would take steps to expel them. But you'd be wrong. The Equal Employment Opportunity Commission is engaged in discrimination claims on behalf of people who have been sacked from jobs they were not supposed to have.

One of the victims of this policy was the Holiday Inn Express hotel. It employed nine illegal immigrants from Mexico who were fired because, it is alleged, they engaged in a successful union organizing drive. You don't really have to be a hard-nosed conservative to find this just a tad strange.

Ma, she's making eyes at me!

If your idea of Nashville is based on girls wearing too many rhinestones, singing maudlin lyrics, you'll be surprised to find that this town is more exciting than you thought.

One of its police officers found himself on the receiving end of love notes from a female officer. She also took as many opportunities as she could to touch him. He claims he complained to senior officers but no action was taken. The female officer admitted to making advances, but claimed that he welcomed them up to the point where his wife found out. The court decided in favor of the molested male and awarded him $200,000 in compensation.

Mouse mismanagement

We have all seen those ads that tell you how you can have an interesting and lucrative career in computers. The "come on" is that it is easy to learn about computers and the favorite phrase is that all you have to be able to do is "point a mouse and click." Why, I wonder, does it never occur to people who respond to these ads that, if that was all there was to it, they wouldn't need to pay computer operators so much money. You could probably train monkeys to "point and click." However, according to the San Antonio Express-News, a dozen students signed up for just such a Microsoft certification course held at the Houston branch of Southern Methodist University. They are now suing because the course was not as easy as they were led to believe. In fact, all 12 of them failed their certification tests and none will be getting a dream job overseeing Microsoft computer systems. "Easy," as they have learned to their cost, is a relative term.

Multiple orgasms

Those who make it their business to advise the rest of us on how to run our sex lives always speak highly of multiple orgasms. Women who have to make do with just one miserable little orgasm are, it is implied, to be pitied.

Now let's turn to the world of telephone sex. I'm sure that you are as ignorant as me about the whole subject. In particular, it has probably never occurred to you to wonder whether the women on the other end of the line are having orgasms or just faking it. Well, here's at least part of the answer. In Florida, one sex worker won damages from her employer for carpal tunnel syndrome (also called "repetitive strain injury"). It seems that in the course of her work, she achieved orgasm up to seven times a day. So, now we have the answer—multiple orgasms are not all they are cracked up to be.

Panhandlers' paradise

Residents of Chicago could be forgiven for being surprised when the city was sued by an unlikely section of the public. Chicago's panhandlers alleged that their civil rights were violated because law enforcement officers ticketed and arrested them for begging on sidewalks. The city settled the action by paying $450 to each of the 3,000 plaintiffs. However, it is expected that attorneys representing the panhandlers are expected to pocket $375,000 in fees which, of course, will also have to be paid by the city. Initially, the city had tried to settle by offering the plaintiffs free clothes. The offer was rejected.

Prying prohibited

A man who applied for a job with a security firm was asked some searching questions and even quizzed about his political opinions. The next thing he heard was that he had been rejected for the job. He sued on the grounds that the company had violated his privacy by, for example, asking about his view on legalizing drugs. The company claimed that the answers to such questions had no bearing on that fact that he was rejected. But the court decided that the prying questions were illegal and awarded the man over $2 million in damages.

Nurses say, "never!"

If you've ever been in hospital, you'll know that nurses are hardworking folks who do their very best for their patients. They often work long hours and the work can be tiring and stressful. But there are limits even for the most dedicated health workers. Six nurses working with disabled patients were fired because they refused to comply with new regulations that required them to give patients "sexual assistance." This involved helping them to masturbate or put on condoms. The nurses are adamant that this is one area in which the patients will have to help themselves and the nurses are suing the hospital.

Cheating, it was

Jared Blair, the manager at a Hooters restaurant, had good news for his staff. He announced a regional competition in which the top ten waitresses from each restaurant would be entered into a draw. The selection was to be made according to who had sold the most beer during the month of April. The prize was to be "a new Toyota automobile."

One of the waitresses at the restaurant, Jodee Berry, 26, decided she would go all out to win. She sold beer with all the energy and enthusiasm she could muster and, in May, Blair told her she'd won. She was blindfolded and led to the restaurant parking lot. However, when the blindfold was removed, she found herself looking, not at a new car, but at a doll in the shape of Yoda the Jedi from the Star Wars movies. Did she find it funny? Oh no. If she'd had a Jedi light saber to hand, Mr. Blair would have been history.

She quit her job and then filed a lawsuit. One of the other waitresses backed up her story. It seems that Blair had kept his promises of what sort of Toyota it would be intentionally vague, but he had certainly given every indication that it would be a motor vehicle. He even told the staff that the winner would be responsible for paying tax on it. Blair claimed that the whole affair was just an April Fool's joke (Toy-yoda—geddit?). But eventually the owners of Hooters settled out of court.

Teacher's trial

Nathan Ganapathi, a 12-year-old student at L'Ecole Bilingue in Vancouver, Canada, filed a lawsuit against his school principal. Luckily for Nathan, his dad is a lawyer so his representation cost him nothing, but the case may end up costing the principal dearly. In Nathan's statement of claim, it said that the principal distributed a letter in which he alleged that the boy was guilty of sexual harassment. It is claimed that the boy said, "You incested your sister" to a classmate. Nathan's remark was overheard and he was suspended from school for two days. Nathan's father said that the principal's letter is libelous and that what was simply profanity has been treated as sexual harassment. He claimed that his son has suffered psychological trauma as a result of his treatment. The lawsuit sought not only an injunction against the principal, but an order that the letter be removed from Nathan's file, and damages for pain and suffering, punitive damages, and court costs.

Chapter Six: Leisure Time

Wipeout!

There is a strict etiquette among surfers. If more than one person attempts to ride the same wave, there is a danger that they will collide and injure each other. This means that you have to signal other surfers that a particular wave is "yours" and no one else should ride it. As in all other areas of life, not everyone is as polite as they should be. So when one surfer took another's wave, the injured party tried to sue. The case failed because the court decided it was impossible to quantify the "pain and suffering" caused by the incident.

A sporting chance?

If you ever collected sport cards, you may be surprised to realize that you were gambling. But this was the contention of Henry Rossbacher, a Los Angeles lawyer, who filed three class action lawsuits claiming that sport card companies are tempting kids to gamble. It seemed that the card producers deliberately printed limited numbers of cards with pictures of the most popular stars to make them more collectable. They also told the kids what the odds were of getting one of the rare cards. This, contended Mr. Rossbacher, amounted to running a lottery and the card companies should pay compensation to the kids who had been inveigled into buying the cards.

A sure bet?

When a woman from California found herself facing gambling losses of over $70,000, she thought of a novel way to correct the situation. She declined to pay her credit card bills on the grounds that internet gambling is illegal. Providian National Bank, just one of the dozen banks and credit card companies she used when placing her bets, sued for non-payment. The woman has countersued credit card companies and online gambling operators on the grounds that internet gambling is illegal in the United States.

Jock jeopardy

A student athlete had a run-in with one of the college jocks and decided to sue. However, he didn't sue his attacker but the dean of his college. He claimed that the same jock had been guilty of other attacks and that the dean should have known that he was violent and taken steps to curb his behavior. The court was unimpressed. It ruled that there was no special relationship between a student on an athletic scholarship and an assistant dean of judicial affairs. The case was dismissed and the dean had his costs paid by the plaintiff.

Baseball battle

This legal tussle started when Barry Bonds, a player for the San Francisco Giants, hit a record-breaking homerun and many of the fans struggled to get their hands on the record-breaking baseball. The Battle of the Ball was won by Patrick Hayashi but only after another fan, Alex Popov, had already caught the ball but had it knocked from his grasp by other fans. It was estimated that the ball was worth in the region of $1.4 million so no one should be too surprised that its ownership became the subject of litigation. At the hearing in 2002, the judge ordered that the proceeds (which turned out to be $450,000) from the auction of the ball be split equally between the pair.

Basket case

Jawann Rubin, a high school basketball player in California, failed to get picked for the varsity basketball team. His father's reaction was not, "Tough luck son, maybe you"ll do better next time." Oh no. Lynn Rubin was made of sterner stuff than that. He filed a lawsuit against the school district claiming $1.5 million in damages and, just for good measure, he wanted the basketball coach to be sacked as well. Lynn maintained that he had put everything into Jawann's basketball career. He had arranged his schedules at great personal inconvenience just to make sure he had time to take his son to practice. He claimed that he had not been consulted about the coach's decision not to promote his son from junior varsity to varsity. The coach maintained that it was school policy that sophomores were restricted to playing only at junior varsity level. Mr. Rubin was not to be pacified. His claim for $1.5 million was based on the potential earnings that Jawann would have made, had he made it into professional basketball.

Basketball rocks!

A man playing basketball with friends fell over some ornamental rocks and suffered minor injury. He decided to sue the owner of the house. One of the injured man's friends was called to testify that not only had the injured man seen the rocks, but had commented on them. The man was adamant that he had not seen the rocks but had to admit that had he looked up, he would have seen them. The case failed as did the appeal.

Blackjack black list

The problem most gamblers have is that they lose their money. It never occurs to them that winning too much could also be a problem. But for Ernest Franceschi Jr. that is exactly what happened. He went to the New York–New York casino owned by MGM MIRAGE and won several thousand dollars playing blackjack. Mr. Franceschi is good at blackjack and wins quite often. This did not suit the casino management who prefer the traditional style of play where the gamblers lose all their money and then leave the casino. It wasn't long before Mr. Franceschi found himself being photographed by casino employees. He left the table but when he came back later to have another game, he was escorted from the casino and told that he was barred from all MGM MIRAGE casinos for life.

But the casino officials didn't leave it at that. It seems that a photo was then circulated to other Las Vegas casinos, presumably with a message warning that this guy was no mug.

Soon Mr. Franceschi found himself unable to get a game of blackjack anywhere. As soon as he sat down at a table, he would be asked to leave. He decided to sue MGM. He wanted $74,000 in damages and also wanted the court to force the company to warn gamblers that they will be barred if they win.

Boomerang bang

Twelve-year-old Jason Davies from Wales was thrilled to be taken on a trip to visit relations in Australia. Imagine his delight when on his first day in the country his dad, Evan, bought him a boomerang. Now, if you ever tried throwing a boomerang, you'll know that getting it to come back to you is not as easy as it looks. Jason read the instruction sheet carefully and then tried his first throw. Nothing. He tried again and again without success. His father and uncle also tried but had no better luck. Then, to everyone's amazement, Jason got the hang of the throwing technique and his boomerang soared into the sky. "Well done, son!" called his excited dad.

Jason turned to give his father a smile of triumph, but in the moment that his attention was distracted, the boomerang swept down on its return path and dealt him a fierce whack on the side of the head, resulting in a cut that needed stitches in the nearest A&E department. The Davies family are seeking compensation from the makers of the boomerang for not including a clear warning that this might happen.

Dicey behavior

When playing craps, it is quite usual for players to ask those standing around watching the game to rub the dice for luck. However, basketball player Dennis Rodman took this too far when he rubbed his dice on the bald head, stomach, and groin of casino dealer James Brasich. Mr. Brasich took offense and sued Rodman, claiming $80,000 because he felt ridiculed by his behavior. Two other casino employees, Rey Novero and Rich Easter, were also rubbed but declined to take any legal action because they did not feel hurt or offended by this behavior.

Fiery feet

Have you ever done a firewalk? The idea is that, after suitable preparation by someone well versed in the technique, you walk barefoot over a bed of red hot embers. In theory, you shouldn't get hurt. Enter Eli Tyler who was attending a convention of the American Association for Nude Recreation in Jacumba. Mr.

Tyler and his friends agreed to take part in a firewalk after being assured that it was safe to do so.

However, far from skipping lightly across the embers with no ill effects, Mr. Tyler suffered some rather nasty burns. He sued alleging that Fred Gilbert, the organizer, had not only used the wrong type of wood but had failed to have the necessary medical personnel standing by. The event had been advertised as "a safe and spiritual experience." The event was held at the DeAnza Springs Resort and the owner is also being sued, though he claims that he warned participants of the danger and got an agreement from them that he would not be sued if anyone was injured.

Fore!

Golf is not usually thought of as a dangerous sport. Yes, sometimes people have stood too close to a golfer and been hit by his club. It has even been known for a player to be struck by a stray ball. This case involves one of the great freak accidents of our time. A woman was enjoying a round of golf when she struck the ball which hit some railroad tracks, bounced straight back, and whacked her on the nose. The normal reaction to such an incident would be an embarrassed laugh, but not on this occasion. The woman sued and won damages of $40,000. Why? Her lawyer argued that the golf club had a "free lift" rule which permits players whose ball lands near the rails to pick it up and throw it to the other side. The argument was that the free lift rule demonstrated that the rails were considered to be a hazard.

Foul play

Baseball isn't all fun and games, as a six-year-old girl discovered when she was hit on the hand by a splinter from a broken bat. She was sitting near home plate at the Tiger Stadium when the incident occurred in 1994. She sued the Detroit Tigers and eventually a jury awarded her $1 million. However, the case went to appeal and the Michigan Court of Appeals overturned the award. It was decided that the baseball stadium owner was not liable for injury caused by projectiles leaving the field, as long as "there are a sufficient number of protected seats to meet ordinary demand."

Gambling with his life

A woman went into a local gambling casino, leaving her infant son locked in her car with the windows closed. The day was a scorcher and kid nearly died from dehydration in the baking hot car. The child's father took legal action not, as you might suppose, against his ex-wife but against the state's gaming commission. Why? Because he claimed that his ex was a gambling addict and the state was supplying her with an addictive drug by allowing legalized gambling.

Golf down under

You might be forgiven for thinking that crazy lawsuits were a purely American pastime but you'd be wrong. Down in Oz, golfers are being warned to take out insurance before they set foot on any course. This is because of a case in which Mark Roy Shanahan was held personally liable for an accident in which a fellow golfer was struck on the head by Mr. Shanahan's ball. The event, held at a Queensland country club, turned into an expensive day out when the court awarded the injured golfer A$2.6 million.

Grumbles on the green

If you have ever hit a golf ball on a regular basis, you will know that there is often tension, not to say friction, between lady golfers and their male counterparts. Many men see their golf club as one of the last bastions of male privilege against the monstrous regiment of women. Naturally, the ladies see things differently. In Boston, the ladies of the Haverhill Golf and Country Club got so tired of the discrimination, they decided to sue. They claimed that the club was not allowing them the best tee times and they were not entitled to full memberships. Not only did the ladies win a massive $1.9 million in compensation, but some of the leading lights of the club were forced to attend gender-sensitivity training sessions.

The odd bit is this: both the ladies and their husbands were surprised to find themselves ostracized by other members of the club. They said they thought that their action would make the atmosphere better but it had actually become worse. Which suggests that some gender sensitivity training might have been of benefit to them as well.

Heckler from hell

Shouting encouragement, advice, and colorful abuse at the players is all part of the fun of going to sports events. How could we enjoy a sporting event without being able to shout witty remarks such as, "Ref, you're blind!"? It wouldn't be the same, would it? But you can go too far. One baseball heckler was so abusive that he was spoiling the game for other fans. They complained and eventually one of the officials asked him politely to be quieter. He refused and tried to bring a lawsuit on the grounds that his freedom of speech had been violated.

Is this a safe bet?

Most of us have bought a lottery ticket or had a little flutter on the horses at one time or another. For most people, it's a harmless amusement but for a minority, gambling is a serious addiction that requires treatment. According to the Wall Street Journal, one addict just could not kick the habit and eventually gambled away his entire life savings and ended up being declared bankrupt. So did he then seek help? Maybe, but not before he'd tried one last desperate gamble: he sued the Indiana casino where he'd been a regular player. He sought $175,000 in losses plus punitive damages. Why? Because he claimed that the casino should have stopped him from gambling. Now, call me naïve, but I thought the idea was for casinos to encourage you to gamble because, after all, it's what they're in business for. If you can't handle that, then you really need to steer clear of casinos all together.

Kournikova confusion

The men's magazine Penthouse thought they were onto a good thing when they were offered pictures of a naked woman on a Florida beach. It looked to them as if the model was none other than beautiful Russian tennis star Anna Kournikova. They started to publicize their scoop and got ready for a really good surge in sales. But then they were contacted by Kournikova who warned them that the photos, taken by a jewelry salesman, were not of her. Ignoring this, they went ahead and printed 1.2 million copies which was double the usual print run.

Apparently, the magazine badly needed a hike in circulation because in recent years its readership had been dwindling. Then they found that not only were they being sued by Kournikova but also by Judith Soltesz-Benetton, the woman who had actually posed for the photographs. The magazine made its apologies and settled out of court. So far so normal. Why is this a crazy lawsuit? Because two attorneys then filed a class action claiming that their clients had paid out $8.99 for the magazine purely for the pleasure of seeing Miss Kournikova with her kit off. The clients, who are both of Russian descent, were disappointed when they discovered they had been ogling the wrong body and they wanted their money back. But why would you file a suit just to get a refund of few dollars? It seems likely that the class action will end up being about much more than the cover price of a magazine.

Mountain mayhem

Climbing is a dangerous sport. You don't have to have much imagination to see that it is very easy to get hurt when you're dangling off the side of a mountain. Fortunately, there are people who are brave enough to rescue climbers in distress. Their efforts, however, are not always appreciated. When a young man was injured in a 90-foot fall, the mountain rescue team leapt into action. A doctor and a paramedic were taken by helicopter at night to attempt a rescue and they managed to save the man's life. You'd expect that he might be deeply grateful but you'd be wrong. He sued and tried to claim $12 million in damages.

Slam drunk?

This is an interesting little problem. Rickey Higgins was something of a star in his high school basketball team. Being a star player has important consequences, with things like college scholarships hanging in the balance. So Rickie was extremely unhappy when he got arrested for driving under the influence of alcohol. This was the second time that booze had landed him in trouble with the law and, as a result, he was kicked off the team. So what was his defense? You might think that, as long as he still played great basketball, his other problems should not affect his place on the team. But that wasn't the argument his lawyer relied on. He sued the school under the Americans With Disabilities Act because Ricky," has been diagnosed as an alcoholic and that is a recognized disability under federal law." The ingenuity of lawyers knows no bounds.

Sore loser?

Anyone who takes part in sports knows that, sooner or later, you'll get injured. Players fall over, sometimes on top of each other, balls fly fast and hard and sometimes make sudden and painful contact with players' bodies. If you want a really safe hobby, you'd be better taking up stamp collecting. Which brings us to Daniel Hannant of Pittsfield, Illinois, who has filed a million dollar lawsuit against Hillerich & Bradsby, the manufacturer of Louisville Slugger bats. Apparently Mr. Hannant was playing for the Pittsfield Saukees against the Calhoun Pioneers when the ball hit him on the head. The blow

was dealt from a hit by an Air Attack 2 Model BB 12 [-5]
Louisville Slugger TPX Bat and now Mr. Hannant maintains that
it could have caused him "serious and life-threatening injuries."
Maybe he should stick to softball?

Sued by a skydiver

What do you think of skydiving? Risky? Dangerous? Downright
perilous? Few would argue with you. When Paul Bloebaum
signed up for lessons he was not thinking of the risk. As he said
afterward, "...I was excited. I thought if I only jumped one time,
nothing could happen. The chances were too small." So he paid
his fee and signed a long waiver agreeing that he understood
the risks and would not sue in case of injury. Not only did he
sign at the bottom of the waiver but he initialed each clause to
show that he had read and understood it. Then he went ahead
and jumped.

Unfortunately, his parachute lines got tangled and he waited
too long to use his spare chute. He suffered a shattered shoulder
and other less serious injuries. What did he do? He sued of
course! Counsel for the Archway Skydiving Center maintained
that Mr. Bloebaum's injuries were not a direct result of the fall
but were suffered after he landed, because he ran across a field

in pursuit of his parachute. The case continued for a lot longer than the skydive did.

Unlucky shot

For anyone not familiar with baseball, Andruw Jones plays for the Atlanta Braves. It is the tradition in baseball, at the end of the third out when the team leaves the field, to toss the ball into the crowd so that some lucky fan will end up with a souvenir of the game. On this occasion, however, a woman in the crowd claimed that she was struck by the ball and, instead of thinking herself lucky, decided to sue. The outcome of her action is still awaited, but in the meantime players and fans alike are sad that what has always been a pleasant custom is now under threat.

Dodging blame

Remember those happy days when you played dodgeball at school? Sadly this apparently innocent pastime is now under attack and may soon disappear from our children's lives for good. The game is now banned in numerous schools throughout the U.S. Why? For two reasons. First, the National Association for Sport and Physical Education has badmouthed dodgeball on the grounds that it encourages violence and harms children's self-esteem. However, the more serious reason is that education authorities think it is only a matter of time before personal injury lawyers start to bring lawsuits claiming that their clients were harmed as a result of their sporting activities. The good news is that there is a move afoot to bring in a Teacher Protection Act that would protect teachers from such claims.

Bowled over

A woman bowler with no previous history of back problems put her back out when she slipped and fell on an icy pothole. At least that is what she claimed. Further investigation showed that she had a long history of back problems stretching back over a decade and she had been treated for a problem the year before her accident occurred. But that wasn't all. Examination of league records kept by the bowling alley showed that she had continued to play during the time she was supposed to be injured. Case dismissed.

Teething troubles

A teenager was going for the greatest of basketball achievements, the slam dunk. He would have made it too, had it not been for getting his teeth caught in the net. Not only did he fail to make the shot but he also left two of his teeth attached to the net. He sued the net manufacturers and the case was eventually settled out of court for $50,000.

Mickey mayhem

Could anyone in the world be more harmless, amusing, and downright American than Mickey Mouse? You'd think that at least this iconic figure, known and loved throughout the world, would be safe from scandal. But now we hear that a California grandmother was taking her grandchildren on a trip to Disneyland when they came upon an unimaginable sight—Mickey Mouse naked! Well, not entirely naked—but the actor had decided to take off his costume and the kids were presented with the awful truth that Mickey is just a guy in a mouse suit. The grandmother is suing for the "trauma" suffered by the kids.

Man or boy?

An African-American university lecturer was working in Norfolk, England, when he started to take an interest in soccer. He decided to go and watch the local team play but when he went to buy his ticket he was shocked and outraged because the man in the ticket booth handed it to him and said, "There you go, boy." The academic—furious that he had been the subject of such a blatant racial slur—tried to hire a lawyer. Fortunately the lawyer was a local man and pointed out that in Norfolk "boy" is a common and affectionate form of address. He was even able to cite a popular song of the time entitled, "Have you got a light, boy?" Women, by the way, are always called "gel."

Chapter Seven:
Famous Faces

Wrong number

A man called Cornell Zachary is definitely not a fan of the band Duran Duran. In fact, he sued them and claimed millions of dollars in compensation. Their offense? Apparently Zachary's phone number had appeared in error on a web site as a hotline for people ordering tickets and merchandise. The poor guy then had to deal with "millions" of calls. He claimed that the whole ordeal had caused "life-threatening high blood pressure episodes." His sleep was also disturbed and he claimed that some of his health problems were permanent. What's more, the number had been left on the web site for several weeks.

Archer's alibi

You may feel that all daft lawsuits happen in the U.S., but you'd be wrong. Other countries have their own way of making the law look stupid. Take the case of British politician Jeffrey Archer. He was the darling of the Conservative Party for years.

His career was dramatic, colorful, and controversial but for many people that just added to his attraction. For example, he recovered from a financial disaster that left him penniless by writing a novel that became a bestseller. He went on to write many more books and became a very wealthy man. But controversy was never far away. In 1987, the Daily Star, a tabloid newspaper with a strong interest in sexual scandal, published an allegation that Archer had paid a prostitute called Monica Coughlan for sex. The allegation would have been enough to destroy his career so he sued for libel.

The court case was also racked by controversy. In his summing up (which is supposed to be a neutral reminder of the facts at issue in the case), the judge persuaded the jury to find in Archer's favor by whipping up sympathy for his wife. He contrasted Lady Archer with the prostitute who was the main witness for the newspaper. Referring to Lady Archer, the judge asked the jury, "Is she not fragrant?" He contrasted the fragrant lady with Monica Coughlan whom he described as "a common prostitute." The jury found in Archer's favor and he was awarded £500,000 ($950,000) in damages.

Many people were appalled at the partisan attitude of the judge but nothing could be done. It looked like a clear case of the establishment protecting one of their own. Now, fast forward to 2001 and Archer (now Lord Archer) was running as the Conservative candidate in the race to be London's first elected mayor. In the middle of his campaign, a former colleague dropped a bombshell that wrecked Archer's whole political career. He revealed that during the libel trail, he had been asked by Archer to concoct a false alibi. Lord Archer was tried for perjury and sentenced to four years in prison. Ironically, the false alibi had actually been fabricated for the wrong date!

Beach Boys blues

It's odd how many times this happens: someone decides in a book, movie, or song to pay tribute to a person they venerate by including a reference to their work. The compliment is often not appreciated and a lawsuit is filed. This happened to the Beach Boys. They had great admiration for Chuck Berry and based Surfin' U.S.A. on his Sweet Little Sixteen. It took a bit of ingenuity to switch the whole song to sunny California but they managed it. Chuck Berry was not that happy about the compliment since it had happened without his knowledge or consent. The case never got to court because eventually a royalty deal and a credit were negotiated.

Bill for compensation?

Rolling Stones' bass player Bill Wyman was peeved to find that there was a music journalist who shared his name. His lawyers sent the scribbler a cease-and-desist letter telling him to stop using the name unless he could prove that it was legally his. He could. However, the Stones' Wyman had no such claim. His real name was William George Perks and he changed it in 1964. By the way, you might like to know that Bob Dylan owes his name to me. When he started out, he was just plain Robert Allen Zimmerman and I threatened to sue the ass off him if he didn't stop using my name. There is also a Robert Allen who makes a heap of money writing books about how to make a heap of money. Now he would be worth suing. Sorry, guys, only kidding!

Bombs away!

Like so many lawsuit stories, this one makes no sense but that does not mean that it isn't true. In 1970, Led Zeppelin had a gig planned in Copenhagen, the beautiful though chilly capital of Denmark. The Danes are famed for their sense of humor (and their ability to hold vast amounts of alcohol). This makes them the life and soul of any party. However, there was one person not caught up in the general jollity and that was Eva von

Zeppelin. You see, Eva was directly related to Count Ferdinand von Zeppelin, inventor of the famous airship bomber. She was not a fan of the band that bore her illustrious family's name, in fact she referred to them as "screaming monkeys" and was ready to sue if they used her name. Why she waited until this juncture to make her threat is a mystery, as the band had been playing for two years already. However, Robert Plant and his fellow band members had obviously been soaking up that famous Danish humor (and not, of course, the alcohol!) and got round the lady's objections by performing under the pseudonym The Nobs.

Brown sings the blues

Kids with a rich daddy usually count themselves lucky. This does not apply to Deanna Brown Thomas and Yamma Brown Lumar, the daughters of soul legend James Brown. They feel that daddy has a grudge against them because he has stated publicly that they will never get a dime from him. Now it may be that Brown just wants the kids to make a life for themselves by their own efforts, but they are determined that the life they want is one that is well lubricated by daddy's cash. They have decided to sue for over $1.9 million on the grounds that he owes them royalties on a couple of dozen songs that they helped him write. They must have been remarkably gifted musicians because some of these songs were written when they were small children.

Chandelier shock

The singer Kenny Rogers once had a brush with the law when he was playing a gig in Dallas. During the gig, Rogers decided it might be fun to throw a Frisbee over the audience. This would have passed off as just a harmless bit of horseplay were it not for the fact that the Frisbee struck a chandelier and broke it. Sitting beneath the chandelier was Kevin O'Toole who got showered with broken glass. Now, unpleasant as this no doubt was, you would not expect it to have any long-term ill effects. A few cuts and bruises should have been the limit of the damage. So imagine poor Kevin's surprise when he found that the shock of the chandelier shower had rendered him impotent. He sued Rogers on the grounds that his wife was deprived of his "services, love and guidance."

Date diddle

In his younger years, Steven Spielberg's career was given a boost by Denis C. Hoffman who plowed $15,000 into his directing efforts. They had an unusual arrangement—instead of taking a slice of the action, Hoffman was to be allowed to choose a project for Spielberg to direct. His choice was to be made within 10 years. By the time the ten years were nearly up, Spielberg had started to make it big. He had directed Jaws and you don't need me to tell you how successful that was. He then claimed that, when he signed the agreement with Hoffman he was only 20-years old and, by U.S. law, a minor. He claimed that his birthday was on December 18, 1947. Later it turned out that he was actually born on that day in 1946, therefore the contract was legal. Hoffman sued.

Dental disaster

Ellen Fein made very few friends when she wrote The Rules which proved to be a bestseller in the 1990s. She urged women to get their man by playing hard to get and to keep him by treating him as, "a client or customer you want to keep happy." Many men and quite a few women condemned her approach as manipulative and dishonest. So it will come as no surprise that there was as a tidal wave of schadenfreude when Ms. Fein came unstuck while having a bit of cosmetic dentistry. She is now suing her dentist because she claims that he gave her "gigantic tombstone teeth" which "deliberately and drastically altered my bite." She complained to the New York State Office for Professional Discipline saying that, "I wake up every morning with teeth and jaw pain as well as pain behind my ears." She claims that it was this dental disaster that led to the breakdown of her marriage. Her dentist, Larry Rosenthal, who is used to working with the cream of New York society, is naturally contesting the case with great vigor. We will have to wait and see whether Ms. Fein will succeed or whether, on this occasion, she has bitten off more than she can chew.

Diamond's danger

In his early days, Neil Diamond was on the Bang label. He had some success there but in the end he fell out with Bang and announced that he was leaving. There was then a very messy period where lawsuits were filed for various reasons. This might have been just another boring litigation tale, but then Diamond's manager phoned to say that he had heard from the FBI that there was a contract out on him because he had messed with Bang. Diamond was understandably scared and borrowed a gun from a friend which he carried with him everywhere he went. He admitted later that he had not the faintest idea what to do with a gun, but until the legal wrangling was over he was not to be parted from it.

Did Nugent say "nigger"?

If Ted Nugent is not a familiar figure to you, then let me fill you in—he is a rocker from Michigan with some unusual opinions. For example, go to his web site and read his fervent praise of hunting. It's just not the sort of thing you get from your average rock and roller. The question is, "Did Nugent go too far?" He has been accused of making racist remarks—a charge he denies—and as a result a concert he was due to give got cancelled. He decided to sue the city of Muskegon (where the concert was to take place), as well as the mayor and Meridian Entertainment who are the concert promoters.

Nugent was interviewed by Rick Lewis and Michael Floorwax for a morning slot on radio station KRFX-FM. They claim that they had to pull the plug on the live interview because the rocker was making racist remarks. It is claimed that he used the words "nigger" and "gook." This incident became known to the concert organizers in Muskegon and they decided that they couldn't let Nugent appear.

Doh!

When you watch TV news, that line of text at the bottom of the screen that gives you the latest highlights is technically known as a news crawl. Matt Groening, mastermind behind The Simpsons, thought it might be fun to imitate the news crawl from Fox News on his show. With his usual gift for satire, he included items such as, "Do Democrats cause cancer?," "Rupert Murdoch: Terrific dancer," and "Study: 92 per cent of Democrats are gay." You get the general idea. Fox, as might be expected, didn't enjoy the joke and threatened to sue. Groening was unimpressed because, as everyone knows, The Simpsons goes out on the Fox Entertainment Channel and he reckoned, correctly, that Murdoch was too shrewd a cookie to waste money having one of his companies sue another.

Don't look now

By all accounts, Sylvester Stallone is not an easy guy to work for. Some years ago, he and his wife were sued by five ex-employees, who had all been sacked for minor infractions of the house rules. One of these was that staff were not allowed to look directly at Stallone.

This reminds me of Anna Wintour, editor of Vogue. Known for her sometimes icy manner, she is often referred to as "nuclear Wintour." This must run in the family because her father, Charles Wintour, a famous British journalist, was known as Chilly Charlie. Anyway, it is said that new Vogue employees are not permitted to address Ms. Wintour until she decides to address them. One new-comer was walking behind her when she stumbled and fell flat on the floor. In a nanosecond, he had to decide whether to help her up, or step over her and pretend he had noticed nothing. He chose Plan B and was relieved to hear later that he had done the right thing, avoiding the sack.

Double-edged compliment

Computer geeks are known for their love of cute names to attach to their products. Who else would have thought of calling a computer "Apple," or describing a little device for pointing at the screen as a "mouse?" When some software engineers (known in the trade as "softies") sought a name for a new piece of software they decided to call it after Carl Sagan, the famous astronomer. To their chagrin, it turned out that Sagan was less than thrilled at being referred to in this way and he threatened to sue. The geeks backed away from the fight immediately (they don't get called softies for nothing) and Sagan was informed that the software was now to be known as BHA. He retired victorious, only to discover that the initials stood for Butt Head Astronomer.

Hair raising

Zsa Zsa Gabor was out driving with her hairdresser when he lost control and slammed into a lamppost. The crimper suffered a bit of shock but was otherwise unhurt. His passenger broke a few bones and ended up in hospital. Now this is the lady who knows the value of everything and who famously said, "I never hated a man enough to give back diamonds." So was she going to sue? Damn right! The case was thrown out however when it was revealed in court that she hadn't been wearing her safety belt.

I don't believe it!

The story so far: Richard Wilson is a famous Scottish actor. He played a character called Victor Meldrew in a long-running British TV series called One Foot in the Grave in which Victor was a retired man who lived with his wife in middle-class suburban comfort. But this was not a story of wonderful "seniors" enjoying their "golden years." The whole point of the show was that Victor was a grumpy, cantankerous old man who was breathtakingly politically incorrect and who would regularly fulminate against everything that was wrong with the modern world (and, trust me, in his eyes everything was wrong). His catchphrase was "I don't believe it!"

Now we can fast forward and find the Caledonian MacBrayne ferry company trying to drum up some customers for its service which links mainland Scotland with the many islands that lie off the west coast. Naturally, this is a popular tourist spot, and the ferry owners included a feature in their brochure "Explore 2004" that pictured the delightful scenery and, more to the point, carried quotes from various famous Scots, including Wilson. Did they ask his permission? No, they didn't. Obviously under the impression that, despite his Meldrew persona, he was at heart a cuddly loveable sort who would allow his name to be used without that elementary courtesy, they went ahead and published. I don't believe it! The case has not yet ended up in court but Wilson has reportedly demanded a contribution to the Scottish Community Drama Association as a way of settling the issue.

Iced

The completely forgettable song Ice, Ice Baby by Vanilla Ice (born Robert Van Winkle) started with a riff that was a straight steal from the Queen/David Bowie song Under Pressure. The plagiarism was done with such outrageous effrontery that no one could understand what had possessed Vanilla Ice to think he might get away with it. The answer was this: yes, he admitted that the two riffs were very close and he hadn't credited the originators, but he had added one note of his own and that should make it fair enough.

Less than grateful

For this story to make any sense at all, you need to know that Jerry Garcia was lead singer with the band the Grateful Dead and died in 1995. While his many fans mourned his passing, not everyone was so cut up. In fact, one attorney in Los Angeles decided that the great man's demise was an opportunity for a joke. He hung a cardboard tombstone in his office and wrote on it, "RIP Jerry Garcia (a few too many parties perhaps?)." Now, though Garcia fans might have thought this in the worst of taste, it does seem to be no more than a silly joke. A fellow attorney failed to see the funny side. It turned out that he was a great fan of The Dead and so he sued. He claimed that the joke caused him, "humiliation, mental anguish, and emotional and physical distress."

Oh, my lord!

People who work in the creative professions live in constant fear of accidentally plagiarizing the work of others. It is not at all unusual for a phrase, idea, storyline, tune, or bright idea to pop into your mind and for it to seem like a product of your own genius, only to find later that it was actually someone else's idea that you remembered. When former Beatle George Harrison wrote My Sweet Lord, it entirely escaped his notice that it sounded very similar to Phil Spector's He's So Fine. Spector sued and Harrison was convicted of "unconscious plagiarism." An even stranger case occurred over the film There's a Girl in My Soup starring Peter Sellers and Goldie Hawn. The plot was about a pretentious food critic whose life is turned upside down by the arrival of a pretty girl. Amazingly, it turned out that at the same time another author had produced a book of the same name with a plot about a pretentious food critic whose life was turned upside down, etc, etc. Strangely the two stories were, in detail, quite different.

Pink pig

The infighting among members of the band Pink Floyd is legendary and, as you would expect from their artistic output, has often had more than a touch of the surreal about it.

When Roger Waters quit the band in 1983, just after the release of The Final Cut, he assumed that the band was about to break up. The others, however, wanted to continue and so Dave Gilmour and Nick Mason began to put together material for what would eventually be A Monetary Lapse of Reason. Waters decided it was time to get a legal ruling over who actually owned the rights to the Pink Floyd name and, of course, the band's assets. After some haggling, Waters agreed that the others could use the band's name but was not willing to let them have the trademark flying pigs. Gilmour is not just a great musician but a shrewd cookie. He simply created new pigs that were easily distinguished from the old ones by their massive balls. The message to his former partner was obvious.

Pop pee

If you've ever been to France, you may have been surprised to find yourself having to use unisex lavatories. Now the French have always had a rather relaxed attitude to peeing, but surely no such thing would happen in the U.S.? Yes, apparently it already has. It seems that Elton John and Billy Joel were giving a concert in the municipal stadium in San Diego. With two such major stars appearing on the same stage, it is easy to see why the event was well attended. There was, however, a down side to the concert's popularity as Bob Glaser was about to find out. He went for a pee and discovered that the men's lavatory had been invaded by women who simply couldn't face the long queue outside the ladies' bathroom. He decided to sue for the "emotional trauma" he suffered.

Posh or not?

Victoria Beckham, now best known as the wife of British soccer hero David Beckham, was formerly a member of a girl band called the Spice Girls. All the girls had nicknames and hers was Posh Spice. Because it is an easy word to fit into a headline, the newspapers perpetuated the name. Nowadays, you only have to glimpse the word from a distance to know that there is another

Beckham story on the way. However, the soccer team Peterborough United is also called The Posh by the fans. Victoria decided that the word was her trademark and sent the team a cease-and-desist. This must have caused David a few problems as he had a foot in both camps. However, after a while, Victoria announced that she was dropping the case and was happy to let Peterborough carry on using the name. It was made to seem as though Victoria was making a generous gesture but it is just as likely that her lawyers had told her she would lose. "Posh" is an everyday word in the U.K. and means "classy." There are those, doubtless a pack of scoundrels, who insist that in Victoria's case the word is used ironically.

Ruined by rock

When Aerosmith were due to perform at an open-air amphitheater called the Concord Pavilion, rock fans thought they were in for a good time. One member of the audience, however, claims that the noise was so loud that he suffered permanent hearing loss. He subsequently claimed compensation for his injuries and lost wages.

Sharon's stones?

When you watch stars arriving at yet another award ceremony, do you envy them all those jewels? If so, you may be heartened to know that they don't actually own them—they're borrowed. It works like this: the jeweler contacts the star and offers to loan her jewels that may cost hundreds of thousands of dollars. In return, when she's interviewed, the star makes sure that she gives her jeweler a name check. She gets the stones, he gets the publicity, and everyone is happy. Well, not quite everyone. Sharon Stone appeared wearing a necklace rumored to be worth $400,000 which had been leant to her by internationally renowned jeweler Harry Winston. However, when the evening was over, Sharon failed to return the rocks. In fact, she was outraged at being asked to give them back because she believed they were a gift. So she sued Winston for $12 million. The case was eventually settled out of court. Sharon gave the jewels back and Winston made a donation to her favorite charity.

So, Madonna, you can't take a joke?

Boy George, former lead singer of Culture Club, was writing lyrics for his musical Taboo. In it he included a send-up of

Madonna's song "Vogue" in which he changed the original lyrics. The new words were, "Ginger Rogers, Fred Astaire, that Madonna dyes her hair." According to him, the whole thing was done as an affectionate joke but Madonna didn't see it that way. She wrote and threatened that unless the song was removed, a lawsuit would follow.

Speak softly and carry a big stick

These days it would take something quite exceptional to make the president of the U.S.A. sue anyone. George W. Bush would be hard put to it to think of a rude name he hasn't been called or a scurrilous accusation that has not been leveled against him during his term of office, but would he sue? No way!

Things were not always so. In 1912, a local newspaper called The Iron Ore carried an editorial about Teddy Roosevelt. George Newett, the owner and editor wrote that Roosevelt, "lies and curses in a most disgusting way. He gets drunk too." Roosevelt was at that time standing for election and he claimed that he rarely touched alcohol, so he sued for libel. The case was heard in the newspaper's home town of Ishpeming, Michigan, and Roosevelt arrived with his whole entourage. He took the stand and verbally thrashed Newett who was forced to retract. Having made his point, Roosevelt asked the court to award him the smallest amount of damages the law would allow. He got six cents—and a great deal of free publicity.

Star Wars

I had always wondered why George Lucas of Star Wars fame was happy for President Reagan to use the name to describe his Strategic Defense Initiative. The SDI (which George Bush would very much like to revive) was an anti-missile system that would use satellites to attack incoming rockets. Naturally, the press liked the name because it was short, catchy, and easily-recognizable. It now emerges that Lucas wasn't at all pleased for his film title to be used in this context and he did try to sue but was unsuccessful. On this occasion at least, "the Force" was not with him.

Stoned

You probably have never heard of Jeff Gillooly, but you will know about his ex-wife—she is Tonya Harding. the woman who was jailed for plotting an attack on Nancy Kerrigan, a figure-skating rival. Gillooly legally changed his name to Jeff Stone and was immediately sued by a whole pack of other Jeff Stones.

One of them was the mayor of Temecula, California, and he claimed that his good name would be "sullied" by association with Gillooly/Stone. The case was thrown out and the new Jeff Stone was allowed to keep his name. Let's hope he doesn't try to make it as a blues singer or he might get sued by Joss Stone as well.

The big hit?

Apparently, actor Mark Wahlberg's reputation for being something of a hard man is not a myth. It is alleged that he once got into a fight with some guy outside the Serafina restaurant in New York and beat the hell out of him. The man sued. So far so normal. But the twist in the tale is this: the guy who got beaten had previously held a job as a bodyguard. The body he guarded? Mark Wahlberg's.

These accusations are garbage

You remember Steven Bing? No? OK, he was the one who was accused of being the father of Liz Hurley's kid. Who's Liz Hurley? Good question. Another time maybe. The point is this: Bing was previously involved in another paternity suit, but then the plaintiff was Kirk Kerkorian, the high-profile businessman.

Kerkorian accused Bing of being the father of a girl that Mr. K. and his ex-wife were raising as their own. The interesting bit is this: Kerkorian had got his hands on some really dynamite evidence: he got hold of Bing's D.N.A. and it matched. But how did he get the DNA? He'd had Bing's garbage raided and had all the used dental floss stolen. Ugh!

Twain's troubles

If I could meet any famous writer at all, I would probably choose Mark Twain. I have more reason than most to be grateful to him. He not only delighted me with his books, but he also single-handedly got me my place in college. At the interview, I was asked to talk about an American author I admired and I waxed lyrical about Twain for so long that they had to offer me a place just to get me out of the room.

I have always thought it sad that the last years of his life were so tragic. Not only did he suffer severe financial loss but he was pre-deceased by both his wife and two daughters. His financial problems were sometimes bizarre. For example, a Canadian publisher brought out a pirate edition of Tom Sawyer. Twain swore they wouldn't pull that trick again so when he was about to publish The Adventures of Huckleberry Finn, he managed to drum up 40,000 advance orders so that (he hoped) he could not be undercut.

The same Canadian publisher had, however, got their hands on a stolen manuscript and they were able to bring out yet another pirate edition. Mark Twain sued them and, for reasons that can hardly be understood, lost.

Unladylike conduct

P. T. Barnum was a man with a genius for showmanship. Many of the tricks of the trade that are practiced today owe their origin to him. In particular, he had a knack for creating interest in areas where it hadn't previously existed.

Take, for example, the case of the Bearded Lady. She was one of the exhibits with the circus and was doing well enough until a dissatisfied customer decided to sue Barnum on the grounds that she was a fake. There was a trial which excited huge controversy. The plaintiff contended that the "lady" was in fact a man in drag. A doctor was summoned to give his expert opinion.

While all this continued, there was an endless stream of customers eager to judge the matter for themselves. It turned out later that the plaintiff had in fact been a stooge planted by

Barnum to create controversy and boost attendance—a pretty good trick, especially if you are the first to think of it.

Vexed vixen

If the name Hunter Tylo prompts you to say, "Who?" then you need to know that she has appeared in a number of highly successful TV series and a few movies. She was all signed up to play a "vixen" in the highly popular TV soap Melrose Place but, before she even appeared in a single episode, she informed the producers that she was pregnant. So they sacked her. They decided that she couldn't play the part while showing off a baby bulge.

One of the things that the show is known for is having a cast of pretty young women who appear showing a sexy amount of bare midriff. The show's web site says this: "What makes Melrose Place so memorable are the little things. Like belly buttons, for instance! Feast your eyes below at the members of the MP Navel Academy."

Tylo, however, was not convinced so she sued and a jury awarded her $2.5 million for pregnancy discrimination, wrongful termination, and breach of contract. Tylo commented, "All I wanted to hear [from the jury] was that pregnancy is not a bona fide occupational qualification... I wanted to hear that, yes, indeed, I could, and can do the job."

Gay Greek?

Probably if I told you that Alexander the Great was bisexual, you wouldn't be too fazed by the news. It's been widely accepted for many years that bisexuality was common and quite acceptable among the warriors of ancient Greece. Not everybody, however, takes such a relaxed attitude to the matter. In fact, many people in modern Greece are infuriated by any suggestion that their national hero was anything other than a "real" man. To them, it's as shocking as to suggest to Americans that John Wayne was in touch with his feminine side.

The issue has been brought to a head by Oliver Stone's biopic about Alexander. Stone tried to get to work on the film for 15 years but, because the Greek government opposed the project, most of the film was shot in Morocco and Thailand. Now, a group of Greek lawyers has launched a legal action designed to force Stone to acknowledge that his film is "a work of fiction." Since Alexander's bisexuality is accepted as fact by most historians of the period, it seems unlikely that the Greeks will get Stone to comply.

This is not the first time that the issue has sparked off a row. Some years ago, hundreds of Greeks stormed an archaeological symposium at which one of the speakers dared to give a paper dealing with the same subject. So great was the hostility of the locals that the police had to be called out to rescue the historians from their wrath.

Too American

If you've heard of a film called Un Long Dimanche de Finacailles (A Very Long Engagement) starring Audrey Tautou, the star of the smash hit French film Amelie, and directed by Jean-Pierre Jeunet with dialogue entirely in French, you might have concluded that it was as French as the Eiffel tower—but you'd be wrong. Because the film was financed by Warner Bros, there were complaints that it was in fact an American film and therefore not eligible for entry in French film festivals. The issue became so heated that it ended up in a lawsuit where the judge decided that it was indeed an American film. C'est la vie.

Great Greek

In ancient Greece the famous dramatist Sophocles had reached the ripe old age of 89 when his son started to suspect that the old man planned to disinherit him. He therefore had the old chap brought before the court in an attempt to prove that he was suffering from dementia. The old man was much smarter than the son had bargained for. He said: "If I am Sophocles, I am not out of my mind; if I am out of my mind, I am not Sophocles." Now if you think about this carefully it doesn't mean much, but it sounds impressive and the court decided in Sophocles' favor.

Chapter Eight:
Feeding Frenzy

You say tomato...

This is an overripe tomato in the eye for all those wiseacres who have used the tomato as the basis of a tricky quiz question. You see, from a technical point of view, the tomato is not a vegetable but a fruit. It may look like a vegetable and turn up raw in salads or cooked in savory dishes, but just because we use it like a vegetable that doesn't alter the fact that botanically it's a fruit. "Ha, ha caught you!" yell the smartasses. But hold your horses. In 1893, Chief Justice Melville Weston Fuller of the U.S. Supreme Court ruled that the tomato may be the ripened ovary of a plant (which is why it is technically a fruit) but as far as U.S. law was concerned, it is a vegetable. Now file that fact away and just wait for the next know-it-all to come along.

Bagel battle

Reuter's news agency reported the case of a couple—John and Cecelia O'Hare of Panama City Beach—who claimed that a bagel had ruined their marriage. When you hear that they bought the rogue bagel from McDonald's, you will be able to fill in the blanks for yourself. Yes, they sued. Is there anybody left in the U.S.A. who hasn't sued McDonald's? The couple claimed that when Mr. O'Hare bit into his bagel, it damaged his teeth and ruined their marriage. Mrs. O'Hare is claiming that she "lost the care, comfort, consortium, and society of her husband." Quite an achievement for one little bagel!

Battle of the barbeques

You might think that, aside from a little gentle rivalry, a barbeque contest would be a happy affair, leaving one clear winner and many pleasantly full stomachs. If you ever go to Johnston, Iowa, you'll find out just how wrong you were.

Jim Woodsmall runs Jumpin' Jim's BBQ and when the judges didn't show sufficient appreciation of his efforts, he got mad. He explains, "I say Jumpin' is my name, and cooking is my game. I compete aggressively." He reckons that success in these contests is the key to his popularity. He alleges that the reason he did so poorly was that the Kansas City Barbeque Society did not judge the entries fairly and failed to follow a uniform set of rules. Apparently, it is not unusual for contestants to complain about the judging but this is the first time it has led to litigation.

So what's your beef?

Did you ever think you'd feel sorry for McDonald's? Admittedly, it's a strange sensation. However, a lawsuit was filed that might cause you to have a twinge of sympathy for the fast-food chain.

Harish Bharti, a personal injury lawyer from Seattle sued McDonald's because he said they misled customers when they claimed to switch from beef tallow to vegetable oil back in 1990. He alleged that they underhandedly continued to fry food using oil with traces of beef in it. He sought a class action on behalf of vegetarians who had been duped into unknowingly consuming beef. He reckoned the damages "will easily be in the hundreds of millions of dollars."

The lawsuit claimed that McDonald's "intentionally failed to publicly disclose its continued use of beef tallow in the cooking process under the guise of 'natural' flavor." McDonald's asserted that they never said their fries were vegetarian and that it was no secret that they used "a minuscule trace of beef flavoring, not tallow." Their spokesman pointed out that 25 million people a day use their restaurants in the U.S. and that none of them would consider the chain to be for vegetarians.

Bharti eventually won his case in 2002, with damages of $10 million and a public apology from McDonald's.

Beer battle

For those readers not familiar with alcohol, you need to know that Anheuser-Busch is a brewery famous for its beer. On the company's web site it boasts: "Welcome to the world of Anheuser-Busch, where making friends is our business!" However, they failed to make friends with at least one of their customers. He tried to sue them. Why? Well, he claimed that the A-B advertising made implicit promises that if he drank their product, he would have success with women. Sadly for him, nothing of the sort happened. He reckons that he suffered physical and mental injury and emotional distress because of the beer's poor performance. The case was dismissed and even though the man took it to appeal, he got no damages.

Buffy's booger

It may seem barely imaginable but there was a time when the name Sarah Michelle Gellar was not synonymous with Buffy the Vampire Slayer. In fact, when she was four-years old, she was the cute and lovable face of Burger King. At that tender age, she couldn't actually pronounce the word burger and used to say it as "booger" (American slang for nasal mucus) and this presumably caused some hilarity.

Her ads were special in another way, too. They actually criticized Burger King's arch rivals McDonald's. Little Sarah Michelle made it plain that she thought little of a Big Mac and would let nothing but a genuine Burger King burger past her infant lips. McDonald's were not amused and sued not only Burger King but also their advertising agent, J. Walter Thompson, and—would you believe it—the cute kid herself. Had they known what a kick-ass chick she would turn out to be, they may have paused before risking a stake through the heart. Ironically, in later years, McDonald's were to go on to sponsor Buffy the Vampire Slayer.

Candy crisis

Do you get annoyed when drivers chuck things out of the window? Of course, it's a dirty and inconsiderate thing to do, but just how dangerous is it? Larry, a cyclist, was going about his business when a van zoomed by and Bob, who was down to the last inch or two of his candy bar, decided to throw it out of the window (which doesn't say much for the quality of the candy). The remains of the candy struck Larry on the leg. Now you'd imagine that, apart from feeling insulted, you'd not suffer too much inconvenience from an accident like this. But Larry insisted that he was so bruised, he had to miss a few days' work. Now, if you think that's a bit of an overreaction, you won't be surprised to learn that he claimed that this candy crisis could have killed him. The court agreed and Bob had to pay damages of $1,000.

Chocolate challenge

Picture, if you will, a Paris strip club in which women wrestlers slog it out in a pit filled with liquid chocolate. One of the wrestlers decided to sue the club. Why? Because of an injury sustained during wrestling? Well, not exactly. She claims that all that rolling around in the brown sticky stuff has put her off chocolate for life. She used to have a healthy chocolate habit like most of us but now she can't even bear the smell. "It makes me sick. After having my face and body covered in chocolate, I can't imagine enjoying it again." She wants $140,000 in damages.

She is not the first to find out that you can have too much of a good thing. New employees of a chocolate company in Norwich, England, used to be allowed to eat as much chocolate as they liked while they worked. They could even buy misshapen chocolates very cheaply to take home to their friends and family. The result was that no one who worked in the factory could bear chocolate and even their nearest and dearest went off the stuff in a big way.

Don't supersize me, comrade

Observers of Eastern European affairs note that while many former Soviet satellite states are adapting happily to life under capitalist democratic regimes, Belarus is an big exception. It is run by Alexander Lukashenko, a former communist who hankers after the old days and, in any case, has no intention of relinquishing power. One of his more eccentric acts was to shut down McDonald's in the capital, Minsk, on the grounds that the food was unhealthy. He proposed instead to set up a chain of restaurants that would sell good, traditional food like cabbage soup and sausages. McDonald's—probably unwisely—threatened legal action. It has obviously not occurred to them that, while in America, if you sue the government then you stand to get compensation, in Belarus you actually stand to disappear quite suddenly.

Don't trifle with Sherry!

Do you like your friends and family to sing "Happy Birthday" to you on the big day? Just about everybody does. In fact, it is so much a tradition that one restaurant in America expected servers to sing it for the customers. However, one of the staff, a lady called Sherry, refused to sing claiming that it was against her religion. She was sacked and the restaurants' lawyers maintained that she had been insubordinate when she refused to obey her supervisor's instruction. The court decided that the restaurant should have made allowances for Sherry's beliefs and found in her favor. She got $200,000 in compensation so, for her at least, it had been a very happy birthday indeed.

Durian disaster

The durian is a strange fruit native to South East Asia. It is about the size of a football and has a thick green skin covered in sharp prickles. Its twin claims to fame are its utterly disgusting smell and delicious taste. This is odd because normally the senses of smell and taste are so closely allied that you would not dream of putting something foul-smelling in your mouth. However, the durian is a notable exception to this rule and is relished so much that some people are more or less addicted to it. It is known in the region as the "king of fruits."

This brings us to the case of a Bangkok resident who was lucky enough to have a durian tree in his garden. Though he was pleased to have a ready supply of delicious fruit so close by, he was obsessed by the fear that passersby might scale the high fence around his property and filch durians from his tree. He bought a number of fierce guard dogs to patrol his property and keep unwanted visitors at bay. All went well until a young boy, intent on getting his hands on a ripe durian, scaled the fence and managed to climb the tree. Apparently, he distracted the dogs by throwing them some nice meaty bones.

All went well until he climbed down the tree with his stolen durian and started back toward the fence. It was at that moment that one of the fruit at the top of the tree was dislodged and fell striking the boy on the head and causing a painful wound. The boy's parents are now suing the tree's owner for the suffering endured by their son.

Kate caught

Everyone agrees that this is a crazy lawsuit but there is plenty of disagreement as to why it's crazy. Here are the facts: Kate (her real name has been withheld) was a 19-year-old freshman at the University of Notre Dame who went out with some friends for drinks at a local bar called The Boat Club. Just after midnight, there was a raid by police cracking down on underage drinking and Kate was arrested, along with over 200 other underage drinkers. At this point, we might pause to consider whether it is crazy to have laws that consider people of 18 old enough for college or, for that matter, old enough to fight and die for their country but won't allow them to drink alcohol until they are 21. But that's how the law stands so we'll leave that point and move swiftly on to the consequences.

The bar was given a choice: it could either have its liquor license revoked (not a great idea if you're running a bar), or pay a $5,000 fine and sell the liquor license to a new owner. Kate, on the other hand, was able to do a deal whereby she paid a fine of $220 and was also given one year's probation. The college also inflicted a separate penalty of 40 hours' community service. She assumed that she was now in the clear and felt that she had got away fairly lightly all things considered.

There was, however, a nasty surprise in store. The Boat Club decided to sue all the kids caught in the raid and claimed $3,000 each. While this is apparently perfectly legal, there has been much discussion of the moral dimension. There are two main opinions: a) Kate and the others used fake ID to involve the bar in an act they knew to be illegal. The bar accepted the ID as genuine and had every reason to sue for the considerable financial loss it suffered, or b) The bar knew darn well that many of the kids were underage and didn't look too closely at their IDs. It was quite happy to benefit from underage drinking until it got caught. You will, of course, pick an answer to suit yourself. There is another option: might it not be time that law makers grew up and allowed youngsters to do likewise?

Let's sue Mom and Pop!

Some people refer to small businesses as "Mom and Pop" establishments. Many of them are small family-owned restaurants. The latest fashion in lawsuits is to sue these businesses for minor infractions of laws intended to make sure that disabled people have adequate access to business premises. Now, let's assume that you are a disabled person and you go to the bathroom in a small restaurant and find that the paper towel dispenser is just out of your reach. What do you do? Bring the problem to the attention of the owners and ask them to get it fixed? Hell no! You find yourself a lawyer and sue the pants off 'em! For some people, this has become an easy way of making money. The owners know how expensive it is to defend yourself against a lawsuit so they cough up a few thousand dollars to get off the hook. In California, the Fresno Bee reported that a lawyer in Los Angeles had recently filed well over 100 lawsuits of this sort.

Mango mistake

In Swindon, England, the local branch of Asda (a supermarket chain) displayed a sign on their mangoes that read: "Their antioxidant properties help to fight cancer." So, the advice is untrue? No, it's perfectly true. What's more the government is enthusiastically persuading people to improve their health by eating more fresh fruit and vegetables. However, there is a rule that prohibits any labeling which claims that a food prevents or cures a disease. Asda was prosecuted, admitted the mistake, and were fined £5,000 ($9,500) plus £1,140 ($2,100) costs.

Milksop

What could possibly be more harmless than a glass of milk? In fact the very phrase "milk and cookies" suggests to millions of Americans the concept of safe, sober enjoyment—but not for Norman Mayo. He sued the dairy industry because he claimed he had become addicted to milk, in fact he described himself as a "milkaholic." He believed that the milk he drank had raised his cholesterol to dangerous levels. He now suffered from clogged arteries and endured a minor stroke. He reckoned that milk cartons should contain health warnings, just like cigarette packets. Commenting on the case Jay Leno, the celebrated TV personality, said, "Here's another reason why Americans hate lawyers." Who knows, perhaps some smart lawyer is already planning to file a class action on behalf of cows whose reputation has been damaged by this case?

Softee suit

You may think that ice cream is not a subject to make you hot under the collar, but you'd be wrong. Mister Softee Inc. got so annoyed with people trading under similar names that they decided to sue. There are mobile ice-cream franchises selling Mister Softee in 15 states. The imitators picked names like Master Softee and Mister Soft. It took some patience to serve the papers on the defendants because they spend most of their time traveling about, selling ice cream. Apparently it is not just the name that is a bone of contention. It is claimed that the rival companies paint their vans in similar colors, too, making customers think they are getting "real" Mr. Softee ice cream.

Movable feast

In America, it's beginning to look as if suing McDonald's is set to take over from baseball as the national sport. Competitors could be given a score based on the sheer wackiness of their lawsuit. Here's a strong contender. John Carter from New Jersey was involved in a car collision with a McDonald's customer. Apparently, the guy had just left McDonald's and was reaching for his carton of fries, when he knocked over a milkshake that landed in his lap. While distracted, he crashed into Mr. Carter's car. According to Carter's attorney, this was the restaurant chain's fault because they should have known that people would drive while eating and should have issued a clear warning that it was a dangerous practice. For once, the court demonstrated some common sense and decided that McDonald's was not obliged to issue customers with blinding glimpses of the obvious. Even so, McDonald's had to pay its own legal fees which came to over $10,000.

Of pesto and passion

It is a measure of just how much the Italians have influenced our taste in food that pesto, which was a virtually unknown foodstuff not long ago, is now appreciated all over the world.

The Genovese sauce made by grinding together fresh young basil leaves, garlic, pine nuts, parmesan cheese, and olive oil is so popular that pasta looks naked without it. And there the trouble starts. Because once something is that popular then everybody wants a bit of the action.

True pesto comes from Liguria and is made with the leaves of young basil plants up to four inches high. Only this sort of pesto can be labeled D.O.C. (denomonazione origine controllata). The first problem arose because the giant food firm Nestlé wanted to get into the pesto market. They produced a version made from basil grown from Swiss and German seeds and it took a lawsuit to stop them calling it "a la Genovese." But that was not the end of the controversy. A report was issued that alleged that the young sprigs of basil contain a chemical called methyl-eugenol. The bad news is that it is a carcinogen and in young basil, it is found in quantities that are 600 times higher than the accepted safety limit. Just to make matters worse, the methyl-eugenol is actually one of the things that makes pesto taste so good. Without it the pesto would be much less delicious.

So, we can no longer eat pesto? Well, not according to the Ligurians. They claim that the cancer scare is a dirty trick to bad-mouth their product to the advantage of those who would sell an inferior pesto made with Kenyan basil and preservatives. They point out that real pesto has been made in the same way for countless generations and so far nobody has expressed anything but total satisfaction with its exceptional flavor. It would seem that the lawyers will soon be in action.

Oral contraceptive

On February 26, 2002, while Ms. Laila Sultan was dining with friends at McCormick & Schmick's Seafood Restaurant, she bit into something of a strangely rubbery consistency in the clam chowder. She removed it from her mouth, only to discover that it was an unwrapped condom. She claims she spent the next 15 minutes vomiting in the restroom. Apparently, the anguish of the experience was so great that she suffered from depression and anxiety for which she needed psychiatric treatment and medication.

Not only did Ms. Sultan file a lawsuit but so did her friends, who had also ordered the chowder. They claimed negligence and intentional infliction of emotional distress.

Sultan says she and her companions placed an order for appetizers, soup, and some drinks. However, when the soup arrived, it was tepid so they sent it back. It was when the chowder returned that she found the condom.

Patrick Stark, attorney for McCormick & Schmick's, was quoted in the Los Angeles Times as saying, "There is absolutely no evidence to suggest the restaurant was the source of the condom, or any employee of the restaurant. Either it came from [the four women] or it was thrown in as a practical joke by another patron at the restaurant."

Apparently, the restaurant manager seized the condom immediately and did not return it to the women. This left an ugly suspicion hanging over the case. As the women's lawsuit puts it: "The condom was possibly a used one." When Stark talked to the Times he said that, because it was rolled up, "it was clearly unused."

Sandwich sensation

That great American invention, the crustless peanut butter and jelly sandwich is under attack. It seems that anyone constructing such a sandwich might now be guilty of a patent violation. Apparently, in 1999, a company called Menusaver Inc. of Ohio was awarded a U.S. patent for a "sealed crustless sandwich. The sandwich includes a lower bread portion, an upper bread portion, an upper filling and a lower filling between the upper and lower fillings, and a crimped edge along an outer perimeter of the bread portions for sealing the fillings there between. The upper and lower fillings are preferably comprised of peanut butter and the center filling is comprised of at least jelly. The center filling is prevented from radiating outwardly into and through the bread portions from the surrounding peanut butter."

Quite unaware of their crime, Albie's Restaurant in Michigan took to serving crustless peanut butter and jelly sandwiches. Then they received a letter from Menusaver telling them that the corporation was going to protect its patent on this iconic American snack. Albie's are not too happy about this and have now asked a U.S. District Court judge in Bay City, Michigan, to give a ruling on the issue.

Pop-Tart peril

If you've never had a Pop-Tart, you're really missing out on a good snack. You just pop one in the toaster and a couple of minutes later a crisp pocket of toasted pastry filled with delicious warm jelly (or chocolate) jumps out and brightens your day. Unless, of course, you are Brenda Hurff of New Jersey. It seems that Brenda put a Pop-Tart—cherry flavor, if you're interested—in the toaster but then left it there while she went to pick the kids up from school. Result? She came back to find that that her kitchen was full of smoke. Did she say, "Silly me, I must remember never to do that again"? No, she sued Kellogg's, the manufacturer of Pop-Tarts and also Black & Decker who made the toaster. She sought $100,000 in damages.

With a name like Smucker's it has to be good. Doesn't it?

Smucker's is well-known maker of jams, jellies, and preserves. In the U.S., the company has been in business since the 19th century and their advertising claims their products, of which they are intensely proud, are "100 per cent fruit." Their slogan is: "With a name like Smucker's, it has to be good."

But are they? A lady in California reckoned that the strawberry jelly she was eating had a slight non-strawberry taste. When the jelly was analyzed, it turned out that only 30 per cent of it was actually made from real strawberries and the rest was made up of fruit syrups and juice concentrates. So now she is suing Smucker's. Whether her claim will prove to be fruitful is yet to be decided.

Snicker doodle democracy

I have to confess that I don't have the slightest idea what a snicker doodle cookie is, so I have no way of knowing whether a gift of cookies would be sufficient to buy my vote. This, however, is the central issue in a strange lawsuit from California.

Julie Ruiz Raber, a councilwoman from the Los Angeles suburb of Carson, gave cookies to all the poll workers in a local election. Her opponent, Vera Robles DeWitt, lost the election by a margin of fewer than 200 votes. She thought that the gift of cookies had exercised an improper influence on the electoral process, so she sued. The judge was not impressed and decided that cookie deliveries did not constitute "electioneering."

Softball girl plays hardball

Cheryl Reeves of Bucks County, Pennsylvania, was hoping to get a softball scholarship but was disappointed. Rather than simply accepting that she wasn't good enough, she is now suing both her coach and the local athletic association. She claims that the coach, Roy Jenderko, taught her a style of pitching called crow hopping. Apparently, this technique is considered "illegal." She also claims that the coach had favorites among the players and this not only harmed her morale but also caused her stress. She sued for $700,000 and alleged loss of future earnings, reputation, and scholarship opportunities.

The McLibel trial

In most of the lawsuits mentioned in this book dealing with McDonald's, it seems that customers sue them over relatively trivial matters like the coffee being too hot. But this case is different because this is one time where the burger chain launched a ruinous lawsuit that did them incalculable harm.

It started with a group of environmental activists called London Greenpeace. This group had campaigned on various issues for years but it was only a small organization. It pre-dated the world-famous Greenpeace International with which it had no connection. In the mid-1980s, they decided to launch a campaign against McDonald's, a company that, for them, embodied many of the things that are wrong with our society. In 1986, they published a six-sided leaflet entitled, "What's wrong with McDonald's?—Everything they didn't want you to know."

At that time, McDonald's in the U.K. was going through a highly litigious phase and suing a number of organizations and individuals who had had the temerity to criticize them. Eventually, they decided to put a stop to the activities of London Greenpeace, but encountered a problem; the organization was an unincorporated association and therefore could not be sued. If they wanted to put a stop to the criticism, they would have to proceed against particular individuals who were members of the group.

They infiltrated the group to find out as much as they could about the workings of London Greenpeace and stored detailed information about the members. In 1990, they threatened to sue five members of the group for libel contained in the "What's wrong with McDonald's?" leaflet. The individuals were told that unless they publicly retracted their criticisms, they would end up in court. The five took legal advice and were told that they could not hope to win a fight with such a large and powerful company. The McDonald's legal team would make mincemeat of them. Because of this advice three of the five decided to apologize. However, two members—postal worker Dave Morris and gardener Helen Steel—refused to grovel and challenged McDonald's to sue them.

Now this is the point at which someone in the McDonald's hierarchy should have sensed danger. What could they achieve by a libel action and how much would it all cost? But in their arrogance, they decided to go ahead and use their legal muscle to crush these people.

The trial turned out to be the most damaging episode in McDonald's history. The British newspapers are mainly of a conservative turn of mind and happily attack environmental activists. But this time it was different. These two British environmentalists, who were conducting their own defense because they couldn't afford lawyers, were being attacked by a huge multinational corporation. Even the greenest of journalists couldn't have failed to see which way the wind was blowing. Obviously McDonald's were going to be the villains of the piece no matter what they did. They were in a hole but they just kept right on digging.

The defendants got massive free publicity for their views. They were regularly quoted in the newspapers and the case was reported all the time on TV and radio news bulletins. They could hardly believe their luck. Their leaflet would have reached a few hundred people most of whom would have thrown it away. Now it was reaching the whole nation and, of course, because McDonald's is a multinational, there was also massive interest abroad. The judge's verdict didn't come until 1997, by which time McDonald's had suffered enormous damage. Worse was to follow. The judge decided that McDonald's "exploit children" with their advertising, produce "misleading" advertising," are "culpably responsible" for cruelty to animals, and are "antipathetic" to unionization. Because the "McDonald's Two" failed to prove all their allegations, they were found guilty of libel and were ordered to pay £60,000 ($115,000) in damages. However, it had long been apparent that these were people with no assets. Trying to get the money out of them would be a pointless task.

If there ever was a crazy lawsuit this was it. If McDonald's had just ignored London Greenpeace, the damage to their reputation would have been minimal. By going to the law, they suffered enormous loss of both money and prestige.

These damages are not peanuts

In Chattanooga, Tennessee, a man was standing on the sidewalk enjoying a snack of peanuts. Unfortunately, he was noticed by a cop who saw him dropping some of the nuts on the sidewalk. Now you'd think that the cop would have satisfied himself by making the man clear up the mess, but not this cop. He decided to take the messy eater for a ride to the police station. As he pulled him toward the police car, the litter lout skidded on the remains of his food and fell heavily, breaking his leg in the process. You can probably fill in the rest for yourself. Yes, he sued both the cop and the city and, of course, he won. The cop had to pay $1,000 and the city's bill was $25,000.

Toastette trouble

Insurance companies are notorious for being unwilling to pay out but sometimes it is hard to believe the lengths they will go to get themselves off the hook. James and Brenda Sticker were making themselves a light snack of frosted fudge Toastettes. You put the snack in your toaster, press the button, and a couple of minutes later out pops a tasty morsel. Except that, in the Strickers' case, the Toastette caught fire and caused serious damage to their home.

You might think that this is precisely why we pay our insurance premiums, to deal with this sort of accident. But no. Allstate Insurance Co. decided to sue Kraft Food (Nabisco's parent company) for $150,000. Lawyers for Kraft Food maintained that Toastettes are not dangerous and that the Stickers must bear a share of the blame for what happened.

Toucan play at this game!

In 1963, Kellogg's, the breakfast cereal maker, introduced a character called Toucan Sam. Sam was a registered trademark and is used to help sell Fruit Loops. A company making golf clubs and equipment called Toucan Gold also uses a toucan (called GolfBird) as its emblem. Kellogg's were unhappy to see a toucan similar to their own being used by another company and so they sued. Eventually, common sense prevailed and the court decided that a toucan advertising cereal was most unlikely to be confused with a bird, albeit of the same species, who advertises golf equipment.

Woman seeks booty

If you have ever come across a snack called Pirates Booty, you may have been encouraged to buy it because it is labeled as low-fat. If you're that interested, you can look the snack up on a web site that tells you everything that's in it. But, this was not enough for one New York woman, according to Newsday. She was lead plaintiff in a class action that demanded $50 million from the manufacturers on the grounds that the snack was mislabeled and, as a result, consumers had to spend extra time in the gym.

A burnt out case

This case starts with three friends going out for a meal at Anthony's Steak House in Geneva, Wisconsin. One of the group, Judge David Schlessinger, ordered his steak medium well-done. Even before the steak arrived, Mr. Schlessinger decided that the service was poor so he complained and demanded better service. When the steak arrived, he thought it was burnt and complained all over again. By this time, the owner of the restaurant, George Condos, was getting fed up with Schlessinger disturbing his other customers. He told him there was nothing wrong with the food and that he should stop making a fuss. Mr. Schlessinger just got more annoyed. He refused to eat the food, pay the bill, or leave. He demanded that a new meal be brought. As that was not about to happen, he used his cell phone to call the police.

It was Officer George Salimes' lucky day as he and another officer were sent to put a stop to the rumpus. Mr. Condos told the police that Mr. Schlessinger might be under the influence of drugs. Salimes told Schlessinger that unless he paid and left, he would be arrested for disorderly conduct and theft of services. So Schlessinger and his friends paid up and left. Is that the end of the story? No way! Schlessinger was only getting warmed up.

He decided to sue, and not just the restaurant, but also Officer Salimes, the Town of Geneva, all the members of the Town Board, the police department, and, of course, the chief of police. He alleged unconstitutional seizure of his person, even though he had not been arrested and had walked out of the restaurant a free man. His lawsuit was thrown out by the courts. But even so Schlessinger tried unsuccessfully to appeal.

Coke controversy

Did you ever notice that Diet Coke from a soda fountain tastes different from the one sold in bottles or cans? If so, did it ever occur to you to sue Coca-Cola? Well, someone thought it was a good idea and the company became engaged in a legal tussle. The issue seemed to hinge on the amount of saccharin used. It was alleged that unless you know the exact amount of artificial sweetener you are consuming, you won't realize that Diet Coke is not as healthy as, say, fruit juice.

Chapter Nine:
Fur, Feathers, and Fins

A Christian act?

Freddy is a guide dog. He was trained by Southeastern Guide Dogs Inc. just outside Tampa. The school trains seeing-eye dogs and supplies them free of charge to the blind. Freddy had only just completed his training and his owner was working with an instructor to get used to his new dog. They decided to get in some practice in the local shopping mall, which is where they bumped into (quite literally) the Christians. Rev. William Christian and his wife Carolyn were out shopping when Freddy's owner accidentally trod on Mrs. Christian's foot and broke her toe. Thirteen months later, the Christian's filed a lawsuit claiming $80,000 each. Witnesses to the incident reported that Mrs. Christian made no attempt to get out of Freddy's way. When asked about this, she claimed that she "wanted to see if the dog would walk around me."

Thoroughly goosed

Being taken to the park, feeding the ducks, and playing on the swings is an essential part of childhood. Darlene Griffin must have had that thought when she took her kid to Okeeheelee Park in West Palm Beach. But instead of feeding bread to grateful waterfowl, she found herself on the wrong end of a rampaging goose. First, the bird tried to attack her son. The little boy suffers from poor health and therefore is in need of more protection than most children. His mother tried to push the goose away with her foot but it bit her. Then it lunged again and this time she fell over backward and cracked her tailbone.

When she investigated, it turned out that the goose had a history of aggression. Video recordings taken after this incident show the goose attacking other visitors to the park. Ms. Griffin acknowledged that she already had back trouble before she got attacked but even so, she sought $15,000 in compensation.

It is not at all unusual for geese to be aggressive. In country areas, farmers would often keep geese near the house because they would scare away intruders more effectively than a guard dog. Plus, unlike a dog, they laid eggs and could eventually be eaten.

Canine's counsel

It is not every dog who can boast his own attorney but four-year-old Boomer from Dayton, Ohio, is an exception. He is suing the Invisible Fence company because when he tried to run through one of their invisible electric fences he suffered second-degree burns on his neck, caused by his collar becoming electrically charged. Boomer's lawyer is the ex-mayor of Dayton, Paul Leonard. While admitting that it is unusual for a dog to have his own lawyer, Mr. Dayton thought that this case might set a precedent. You will be unsurprised to hear that The Invisible Fence company is not thrilled at the idea. Their lawyer is quoted as saying, "Under Ohio law, animals are considered personal property of the owner, and our research indicates that animals can neither sue nor be sued."

Cat claim

Venus Viola was, according to her owner, Lamar Peoples, no ordinary cat. She was extremely beautiful and, more importantly, her owner reckoned his cat brought him luck. Venus Viola's luck ran out when Mr. Peoples' wife Marie decided to take the cat to work with her at the Northampton State Hospital. Cats are notoriously curious so it wasn't long before Venus Viola was taking a close look at the hospital grounds. She was unfortunate enough to touch a live wire and get electrocuted. Mr. Peoples decided to sue the Massachusetts Electric Company.

He claimed over $200,000 in compensation, plus veterinary bills and, most controversially, $250,000 which the lucky cat would have brought him had she lived. Naturally, the electric company was not impressed by the cat's earning power and contested the case. A judge advised Mr. Peoples to settle out of court.

Dirty dog

One issue that is guaranteed to get neighbors at each other's throats is that of dog poop. Doesn't it just drive you crazy when someone lets their dog crap all over the place? This brings us (unwillingly) to the case of Shiner, a dog owned by Rick Heckman, a resident of Leonia, New Jersey. It seems that Shiner was a dog on a mission. He decided to poop on the grass verge belonging to William Ramos. Mr. Ramos was not happy. He filed a lawsuit on the grounds that Heckman was in contravention of the town's code on disposal of canine waste. He claimed that, as the owner of the land, he should have been asked for permission before the dog was allowed to do its business. The central issue was whether Mr. Ramos actually owns the land. He claimed that he did because the town required him to mow it. Mr. Heckman felt that if the case went against him, it would be the end of dog walking as we know it. Apparently, no one has taught him the little trick with a plastic bag that allows you to remove your dog's poop and dispose of it properly.

Fowl temper?

Like many other people, Marian and Chuck Butler from Florida enjoyed feeding the birds in their garden. They enjoyed it so much that they would buy 40 pounds of seed each week to lavish on their avian friends. Their neighbor, Edward Renna, was not as keen on the birds as the Butlers because he found that they were leaving their droppings in his yard. For years, he would try to scare the birds away. Whatever he did, they still managed to attack his fruit trees and leave droppings on his boat. Eventually, he tried for an injunction to stop the bird feeding. He also wanted $5,000 to compensate him for the damage caused by excessive guano. The case went before Judge Peyton Hyslop who concluded that although it was likely that the Butlers had contributed to Mr. Renna's problem, there was no proof that bird feeding was the sole cause. He was awarded no damages and both sides had to pay their own costs.

Goose gang

Nolan Lett had just started a new job for Aramark Corp, a catering company in Oak Brook. On his second day, he was sent on an errand that included using the building's side door. As he emerged, he was attacked by a pair of Canadian geese. A goose attack is no laughing matter as the birds are large and can be extremely aggressive. Nolan decided that his best bet was to get back into the building but, as he tried to do so, one of the geese leapt at him and he had to struggle to push it away. The struggle became so heated that Nolan fell over and broke his arm. He sued and was paid almost $18,000.

Having a whale of a time

Just when you think that lawsuits can't get any crazier, you find one that makes that leap from crazy to surreal. This one begins with the discovery at Sea World in Orlando, Florida, of a naked man lying dead on the back of a killer whale. The man, Daniel Dukes, 27, was a drifter who had apparently slipped past security guards and drowned while attempting to swim with the killer whale. His parents, Michael and Patricia Dukes, decided to sue and claimed millions of dollars for the emotional distress caused by the loss of their son. Their attorney, Patricia Sigman, contended that Sea World was liable because they encouraged the public to believe that the whale was friendly to humans. No notice had been posted warning people not to swim with the whale. Now, some of us might have been put off by the name "killer whale." While we know that these creatures do not normally attack humans in the wild and confine their killing to seals and suchlike, even the bravest of us might think long and hard before diving into a pool and keeping company with a whale. But since when has common sense had anything to do with the law?

Hot dog

Dorothy Johnson had a dog; she also owned a microwave manufactured by Kenmore Inc. How are these two facts connected? It happened when she gave her dog a bath. She decided that drying the pooch would be quicker and easier if she gave it a quick spin in the microwave. She left it in, "just a few minutes on low." This was too much for the poor pet which came out medium rare and quite dead. Ms. Johnson attempted to sue the makers of the oven but her case was thrown out. Let's hope she's learned her lesson and in future only warms her dogs gently on defrost.

Library cat booked for assault

If you ever find yourself in Escondid, CA, and fancy a trip to the library, beware! The library cat is not one to be messed with as Richard Espinosa found out to his cost. He went there with his dog Kimba, a 50-pound Labrador mix. He alleged that the cat attacked his dog, causing wounds that cost him nearly $50 of veterinary bills, plus nearly $40 of chiropractor's bills for his own injuries. Mr. Espinosa filed a claim against the city for $1.5 million. What's more he demanded that the library should give proper warning and, just to make sure, the cat should be de-clawed.

Mr. Espinosa was quoted as saying that he suffered, "significant lasting, extreme, and severe mental anguish and emotional distress including, but not limited to, terror, humiliation, shame, embarrassment, mortification, chagrin, depression, panic, anxiety, flashbacks, nightmares, loss of sleep, (and) loss of full enjoyment of life, as well as other physical and mental afflictions and pain, suffering." Apparently, Kimba was more than just a pet, he was a trained assistance dog who helped his owner deal with panic and anxiety attacks.

Rodeo rage

Kids from Bay Area in San Francisco were due to be taken to a free Grand National Rodeo day being held at Cow Palace. The teachers had reckoned without parent Peggy Hilden, mother of Collin. She held the view that rodeos violate animals' rights and claimed that the California Education Code supports her stance. The code forbids schools from teaching or encouraging the inhumane treatment of animals. It was also claimed that seeing violence inflicted on animals might upset the children.

The lawyer and the snake

Do you know why snakes never bite lawyers? Professional courtesy. Now that is just the sort of smart Alec remark to get American lawyers riled. So you can imagine just how annoyed a California attorney was to find her name had erroneously been included in the telephone directory under "Reptiles." Everyone had a really good laugh about it. There were snide remarks in newspapers and even Jay Leno got in on the act and made fun of the unfortunate attorney. Did she take it all in good part? Did she heck! She sued claiming $100,000 in compensation from the phone company.

Blind to his faults

A blind man was perfectly happy with his guide dog, until the day that it led him to bump into a woman. It is alleged that he stood on her foot causing her injury. The woman didn't sue the blind man but filed suit against the school that trained the dog.

Pink porker?

A Bulgarian farmer went to market to buy himself a pig. He picked out one that looked fat and healthy and would help him to breed some fine livestock. At first all seemed well, but when he tried to mate the pig he had no success. None of the sows seemed to take his fancy. The farmer couldn't work out what was wrong so he consulted the local vet. The pig was examined and given a clean bill of health. Eventually, he found the root of his trouble—his pig was gay. He decided to sue, claiming substantial damages.

Cat confusion

In Suffolk, England, Elsie Greene (83), had lived in happy companionship with her tabby cat, Suki, for many years. True, Suki had a habit of wandering off for a couple of days at a time, but she always came back in the end and resumed her life of domestic bliss with Elsie. However, one day, during one of Suki's unexplained absences, Elsie was invited to tea with another elderly lady who lived nearby. She was astonished to find Suki stretched out in front of the fire. Apparently in her second home she was known as Toto. It was the first time that either "owner" was aware of the other. Now they could have laughed about the mix up and agreed to share the cat but instead they fell out over it and consulted lawyers. Suki/Toto settled the matter out of court by managing to get run over before the case came to trial.

Rooster ruckus

When James Sherwood and his family moved to the Surrey countryside they hoped for fresh air, open spaces and a little peace and quiet. What they got was the smell from a neighboring pig farm and the noise of the local rooster that woke them bright and early every morning. They tried to get the smell reduced and the rooster butchered but the farmer wasn't helpful. In fact he told them that if they didn't like the country they should go back to the city where they belonged. The matter went to court and the judge told the Sherwoods that the farmer was right. Live next to a farm and you needn't be surprised if you get smells and noises.

Chapter Ten:
Zany Behavior

Winnebago warning

A Winnebago motor home is an impressive vehicle. They're 32-feet long and built like a bus. You would imagine that anyone in the driving seat would take great care where they were going. But you would be wrong.

Take the case of Merv Grazinski from Oklahoma. He'd just bought a brand new Winnebago and was taking it on a trip. He got as far as the freeway and felt the need for a cup of coffee. Did he stop at a roadside café? Hell, no! He set the cruise control at 70 mph and walked to the back of the vehicle to make the coffee himself. What happened next will come as no surprise. The vehicle ran off the road and overturned. Now, you may have expected this outcome but Merv didn't. He thought that the makers of the Winnebago should have warned him that he couldn't leave the vehicle unattended while driving. He sued and a jury awarded him $1,750,000 plus a new R.V.

A grave offense?

A woman in Oregon was giving a family friend a lift to visit the local cemetery. She had her 13-year-old daughter in the car with her. It seems that she had had a little alcohol—not enough to make her really drunk but just sufficient to rob her of her better judgment. Realizing that she was off the public roads, she offered her daughter a driving lesson. The kid apparently accepted the offer with alacrity and took control. Unfortunately, her enthusiasm outstripped her ability and she plowed into some of the tombstones. By the time the car came to a halt, she had badly damaged three tombstones and knocked bits off a dozen others. The police arrived and arrested the mother. Given the litigious state of U.S. society, how long do you reckon it will be before the relatives of those whose tombs were damaged file lawsuits? Probably it will be quicker than you can say, "R.I.P."

A twisted tale

You have probably seen the psychic Uri Geller perform his spoon-bending feat. He's been at it for years and has performed all over the world. No matter how many skeptics cry "foul," there is never any shortage of people who confess themselves to be intrigued and mystified by his apparent ability to cause solid metal objects to become mangled. Many claim that not only does he perform these feats on purpose but that, on occasion, they occur in his vicinity whether he likes it or not.

Geller, though Israeli, lives in the U.K. and was invited to meet the Lord Mayor of Liverpool. The dignitary was done up in all his finery including a really nifty ceremonial gold chain of office. To his amazement, he found that after shaking hands with Geller, the chain had become twisted completely out of shape. This prompted the press to ask Geller what was the most unusual example of such a thing happening. He told them that one lady had threatened to sue him because while she watched his performance on TV, her contraceptive coil had become twisted and she subsequently became pregnant.

Arrears

Danielle Kousoulis was a successful career woman who had worked her way up to be vice-president of Cantor Fitzgerald. She worked in their office in the Twin Towers and was one of those tragically killed in the terrorist attacks on the buildings on September 11, 2001.

Just before she died, she had signed a lease on a new apartment. After her death, her landlord decided to sue on the grounds that she was in arrears with her rent and had not given the necessary three months' notice that she intended to quit.

Best of three

New Zealand has a reputation for being a bit traditionalist. Some people unkindly describe it as "like the U.K. in the 1950s" which is probably a vile slur on a beautiful country. It is true, however, that they have their own way of doing things. For example, two companies were involved in a dispute over access to a mobile radio network. The C.E.O. of Teamtalk and the chief exec of M.C.S. Digital drew back at the last minute from settling the whole thing in a potentially expensive lawsuit and agreed to sort out their differences in a best-of-three arm wrestling contest.

Blender blunder

You know that corny old sight gag from the movies where someone pulls out the bottom object from a stacked pile and they all fall down? Pure Laurel and Hardy, isn't it? No one would ever actually do it, would they? Well, yes, it seems they would.

Enter Janette Weiss, a part-time cafeteria worker. She visited Kmart to buy a new blender and, for reasons we can only guess at, decided to pull the bottom box out of the display. You don't need a college diploma to work out what happened next. The whole pile fell on her. She sued Kmart claiming that it was their fault that she suffered pain and carpel tunnel syndrome. The case rumbled through the courts for three years but finally a jury came down on Ms. Weiss's side. Kmart paid compensation.

Bombing Auschwitz

In recent times there have been many lawsuits filed by Jewish survivors of the Holocaust who have attempted to get Swiss banks, some German companies, and others to pay for their part in the attempted genocide. Now, however, there is a new and much more startling claim. Two Holocaust survivors, Kurt Julius Goldstein and Peter Gingold are plaintiffs in a class action which is demanding $40 billion in compensation for the survivors and descendants of those who died in Auschwitz. They are suing the American government for failing to bomb the concentration camp. Their contention is that had the place been bombed, it would have saved the lives of 400,000 Hungarian Jews who were later interned there.

Reaction to this case has so far been unfavorable. Michael Berenbaum, who wrote a book entitled The Bombing of Auschwitz commented, "This is silly and ridiculous." He also asked why the plaintiffs weren't suing the German government that had actually built the camp.

Although their case was thrown out of court in 2001, the lawsuit continues to be pursued and there is no sign yet that the plaintiffs are in any mood to give up.

The Bride of Wildenstein

There are few lawsuits stranger than the divorce proceedings of society diva Jocelyne Wildenstein and her husband. Mrs. Wildenstein was born into a middle-class family in Lausanne, Switzerland. At an early age, she decided that fate had played a dirty trick by not placing her in a wealthy family and she set out to remedy the situation.

She was very pretty and knew that her looks could provide a passport to the sort of life she wanted. She took a great interest in hunting and learned to fly light aircraft. It was these attributes that earned her an invitation to a shooting weekend at the vast Kenyan estate of Alec Wildenstein, the heir to a $10 billion art fortune. He was very impressed, not only by

Jocelyne's lion hunting ability, but also by her beauty and personality. When she returned to Paris, she found her new admirer had sent huge bouquets of orchids as a mark of his admiration. Their relationship prospered and within a year they were married in Las Vegas. The new Mrs. Wildenstein moved into to Alec's apartment on Park Avenue and began the life she always knew she was meant for—as a society wife.

While her husband continued to run his art business and his Kenyan estate, Jocelyne busied herself looked after their many houses around the world. In France, they had a chateau in the country and an apartment in Paris. They also owned a Caribbean estate and, so that Jocelyne could be close to her family, they bought another estate in Lausanne. Their main home was a luxurious house in New York.

Jocelyne had a weakness for exotic animals and it was this that was eventually to be her downfall.

Her position in New York high society was harder work than you might expect. She was constantly having to acquire designer gowns and expensive accessories in order to keep up appearances. Her husband not only footed the bill for these but also lavished $10 million on buying her jewelry. However, marriage does not always run smoothly and even the most affluent and privileged have their problems. Alec Wildenstein suffered from bouts of depression and, though Jocelyn tried her best, she wasn't up to the task of lifting his mood. Then only things that gave him constant pleasure were the lions that he kept in a private jungle and his art collection.

Eventually Jocelyn suspected that Alec's eye was roving and it was time for her to do something to recapture his attention. She was now in her late forties and thought that a bit of plastic surgery might restore her physical charms. The first operations were a great success and it seemed for a while that the couple was once again in love. Eventually, however, her old doubts resurfaced and Jocelyn dreamt up a desperate plan to recapture the affections of the man she loved.

She once again visited a plastic surgeon and asked him for something a little out of the ordinary. She wanted to look like one of the big cats that Alec was so fond of. She felt that if she resembled one of his beloved wild creatures, she would be sure of his love and attention. The plan required a huge number of operations but, in the end, Jocelyn got what she wanted. Not only was her face remodeled to resemble that of a big cat, but she had her skin pigment darkened to add to the dramatic effect. Sadly her plan did not have the desired effect. To say that she looked scary would be a great understatement. In fact, it was reported that the first time her husband saw her new face, he screamed with shock. In spite of all her efforts, the couple separated and a long, messy, and acrimonious divorce ensued.

Carousel capers

Wal-Mart Stores Inc is a massive supermarket chain with interests throughout the world. Just because they're big, it doesn't mean that they ignore small issues. For example, they have a carousel device that holds blue plastic shopping bags. The cashier can drop the items into a bag as the items are rung up then, when the bag is full, the carousel can be turned so that the customer can pick up the bag. Wal-Mart are so pleased with this neat little device that they have patented it, and this is where the trouble started.

Kmart is a rival chain and they have similar carousels in some of their stores (they claim it is fewer than 20 carousels in over 1,500 stores). Nevertheless Wal-Mart is suing Kmart for violating its patent. Kmart insist that their carousels include scales that weigh the items and, because the Wal-Mart ones do not have scales, they can't be the same. You may well think that this is a foolish argument that should not be taking up the time of grown men and women (not to mention the courts). But it is a safe bet that this is a battle that will be fought vigorously.

Drunk and dangerous

In Florida, a man who'd been enjoying himself with a few drinks decided it would be a good idea to climb up an electrical pylon. To get to it, he had to climb over a fence and get past a locked gate. This he did—it's amazing what you can do when you've had a few—but he was injured while climbing the pylon. He sued half of dozen of the bars, some liquor stores, and the electric company.

Eenie meenie

Louise Sawyer and her sister, Grace Fuller, were taking a Southwest Airlines flight. It may be that passengers were a taking a little too long to get settled because a flight attendant was heard to announce, "Eenie, meenie, minie, mow, pick a seat we gotta go." The sisters decided to sue. Why? Well, if you are of a certain age, you will remember that the second half of the original rhyme was not about airplane seats but ran, "catch a nigger by his toe, if he hollers let him go, eenie, meenie, minie, mow." It is quite doubtful whether the airline attendant or most of the passengers were even old enough to remember the rhyme since it has long been consigned to the trash can of political incorrectness. Even so, the sisters felt that a grave insult had been offered and compensation was due.

Eruv over our heads

Unless you're an Orthodox Jew, you could be accused of thinking that the title of this piece is an unfortunate misprint. If you're thinking, "What the heck is 'eruv' supposed to mean?" you will not be alone. However, the concept of an eruv is of the greatest importance to those who choose to obey to the letter the very strict and complex rules of the Jewish religion. By tradition, on the Sabbath there are certain things that orthodox Jews cannot do outside the home. For example, work is forbidden. That might seem no great problem but, in this context, it would include things like pushing a wheelchair or even carrying certain items. It is easy to see just how restrictive this would be. There is, however, a loophole. It is allowed for a whole area that takes in many Jewish homes to be designated as an "eruv." In effect, it makes this public space an extension of private homes and therefore a variety of necessary activities can be carried out without violating the religious law. So far so simple—but this story is not simple at all.

In London, there are a number of areas with a large Jewish population. This takes in neighborhoods such as Golders Green, Hendon, Hampstead Garden Suburb, and a bit of Finchley. Many of those who live there are Orthodox Jews and they called on their community leaders to have the area classified as an eruv. In theory, nothing could be simpler. To make an eruv, you need to have clearly defined boundaries. Fortunately, this area is bounded on one side by the M1 motorway and on another by the Northern Line of the London Underground—but how to define the third side was the problem. Along the 11-mile boundary there were 34 gaps where, for example, roads penetrated the eruv. Traditionally, you can get over this by creating gates known as "tzures hapesach." To create the "gates," you need to erect a series of tall poles connected at the top by thin wire. In this case, they needed 82 poles. This "fence" is not very obtrusive. In the jungle of lamp posts, phone wires, power lines, traffic signals, and boards giving directions to drivers, some new posts and wires would be barely noticeable.

This is where the insanity kicks in. You can't go erecting posts and wires without planning permission. When the Jewish community asked to be allowed to create their eruv, there was an outcry. Some of the fuss came from locals who felt that the area was being "claimed" by the Jews. These people were in a rather tricky situation because what they were saying seemed to be only a hair's breadth away from racism. Had they been alone, it is unlikely they would have had much effect. Like any other civilized society, the U.K. doesn't take kindly to racism. The more perplexing problem was that Jews belonging to reformed or liberal congregations saw the eruv as a maneuver by their Orthodox neighbors to inflict on them restrictive rules that they didn't want. This is something the Orthodox community denied absolutely. They maintained that the fencing of the eruv sent a clear message to them and to no one else.

Scare stories to the effect that some of the poles would be erected in people's gardens circulated. Again, this was dismissed as untrue. Some people might have a pole outside their garden but that was no different to having a speed limit sign or a telegraph pole. What is called "street furniture" will always be near to someone's house.

Eventually, the eruv boundaries were agreed and the area was marked according to the requirements of Jewish law. This could be seen as a victory for common sense and the British art of compromise. But the whole stupid unnecessary quarrel had taken 13 years to resolve! What can you say? "Oi vay!" might just about cover it.

Faulty forecast

In the U.K., the highly changeable weather is a source of endless fascination. In any one day, you might have snow, rain, and sunny spells. The temperature goes from hot to cold in a matter of hours. Because of these rapid changes, the weather forecast is treated with amused skepticism. Not so in Israel, however. A woman there decided to sue a TV weather forecaster who predicted sunny conditions when, in fact, the day proved wet. The woman went out dressed for a nice warm day and got soaked. She reckoned that this unscheduled shower caused her to catch flu, miss several days off work, and pay out for medication. She asked for $1,000 in compensation.

Fiancé fury

At one time, a gentleman had to think carefully before breaking off his engagement because there was a chance that he might be sued for breach of promise. But all that's over now, right? These days an engaged couple who split just go their own ways and start over with someone else. But that is not always the way it works out. There was a case of a woman who sued her former fiancé even though the engagement had lasted a mere seven weeks. Amazingly, she won $178,000! She got $93,000 for pain and suffering, $60,000 for loss of income, and $25,000 for bills run up during psychiatric counseling. The unfortunate man had to console himself with the thought that things could have turned out worse—he could have married her.

Firework fiasco

What could be nicer than spending the Fourth of July at home with your folks letting off a few fireworks? One man did just this but he also had quite a lot to drink. He then lit one of the fireworks he'd brought with him. As sometimes happens, it failed to go off. Now, you no doubt remember the safety instruction for using fireworks. You never go back to inspect a firework that hasn't ignited. What did our hero do? Yep, he went back to see what was wrong and the firework exploded in his face. Did he say, "What an idiot I was to do something so stupid?" No, he sued his parents, the person who sold him the fireworks, and his employer.

Flight fury

This story starts with a lawsuit that was conducted by lawyer Arthur Alan Wolk against Cessna, the aviation company. The proceedings were reported on a web site called AVweb (an internet aviation magazine). Having won a huge victory in which Cessna were ordered to pay $480 million, Mr. Wolk then proceeded to sue AVweb, some of its editors, and subscribers with a lawsuit in which he claimed $100,000 in compensation and punitive damages. Why? Well, it seems that the case prompted some sharp criticism of Mr. Wolk in the course of which he was called, among other things, "a self-promoting ambulance chaser." AVweb are now asking readers for donations to help pay for their defense.

Flying farce

Have you ever thought it might be nice to be able to levitate? It would be handy for getting around without becoming stuck in traffic. It might also impress members of the opposite sex. In fact, it would revolutionize your whole life. This might explain why one man joined a group that promised to teach levitation. He spent time bouncing around on his butt before realizing that he was doomed to failure. He sued the group and sought damages of $9 million for the physical and psychological damage he had suffered.

Foundation failure

A heated disagreement in San Antonio, Texas, led to a surprising conclusion. First, one of those involved rammed the house of the couple he'd been arguing with. He made such an impact that the house was knocked off its foundations. This left the couple with a problem. The man had no money and was not worth suing. What to do? Then they had a bright idea. They sued the engineer who was responsible for the foundations. Even though his design was within the specification demanded by the San Antonio building code, he was still ordered to pay damages of $40,000.

Good vibrations?

Picture yourself on a plane in Dallas awaiting takeoff. Suddenly someone calls your name over the PA system and you are promptly taken off the plane by airport officials and asked to open one of your pieces of luggage. So far, so embarrassing. But imagine how you'd feel if, when you displayed the contents of the bag, it turned out that you had included a vibrating sex toy among your belongings. Just how embarrassing would that be? All this actually happened to a woman who had bought the toy in Las Vegas. The airline officials had become suspicious because they could hear something vibrating inside the bag. The woman's humiliation was made worse because she had to hold the toy up for everyone to see. Even passengers on one side of the plane could see quite clearly what was going on and, apparently, three male Delta employees couldn't keep from laughing.

After all the humiliation, the woman was allowed back on the plane. At first, it seemed that she just wanted to forget the story—at least, that is what she said when interviewed by a journalist. But she must have had second thoughts because she filed a lawsuit and, of course, the story received maximum publicity.

Handyman

Usually you would take special care using power tools. You might wear goggles to protect your eyes, ear defenders to prevent hearing loss, maybe even a pair of gloves to dull the effects of vibration. However, none of this sprang to the mind of an American man who used a chainsaw to cut off his own hand. If his behavior seems strange, the reason he gave for it was even stranger. He claimed that the hand was possessed by the devil. He was rushed to hospital where doctors managed to stop the bleeding, but when a surgeon offered to reattach the hand, the patient told him that it was against his religion. Now we get to the really strange bit. He later tried to sue both the surgeon and the hospital on the grounds that they should have realized he was psychotic and therefore should have ignored his protests and operated.

Happy birthday? Nope

Ask anyone and they will tell you that the song "Happy Birthday to You" is a traditional song for which there is no copyright. But they will be wrong. The copyright actually belongs to Warner Music. Irving Berlin found this out to his cost when he included the song in the musical As Thousands Cheer.

Apparently, the rights to the song are worth a couple of million bucks per annum, which is why Warner take it so seriously. But don't get worried—apparently you are allowed to sing it at family parties free of charge. Incidentally, I bet you didn't know that the song is actually quite difficult to sing properly. It is often used as a test piece for auditioning singers because there is a difficult note in it that only a really good singer will get right.

Health hassle

Do you know what things to do to improve your health? Unless you are recluse or a complete lummox, you will have heard it all a thousand times before. Lose weight, don't smoke, check your blood pressure and cholesterol, take some exercise, cut out fats and sugars, but eat lots of fresh fruit and vegetables. None of this would be any news to you. Not so Kathleen Ann McCormick. She was obese and a smoker with high B.P., high cholesterol, and a history of coronary heart disease in her family. She visited the Veterans Affairs Medical Center and was seen by doctors. What did they tell her? What do you think? Is it remotely likely that they said, "Keep eating and smoking Kathleen and you'll be just fine?" I think not. Eventually, she had a heart attack and filed suit because she claimed that her doctors had not done enough to help her improve her health. She tried to claim a million dollars from the doctors and the U.S. government who employs them.

House of horror

When Cleanthi Peters took her 10-year-old granddaughter to the Universal Studios' Halloween Horror Nights in Orlando, Florida, they made straight for the haunted house in search of a little scary fun. They got a bit more than they bargained for when, as they approached the exit, they were chased by an employee wielding a chainsaw. The chain had been removed from the saw but that was not a detail they had time to consider. Instead, they did the obvious thing and ran like crazy. Unfortunately, a wet patch on the floor caused them to slip and fall. They claim that the employee, far from helping them up, continued to threaten them with the saw. They not only suffered unspecified physical injuries but also suffered "extreme fear, emotional distress, and mental anguish". They sought $15,000 in damages.

Insane Clown Posse

If you have never heard of Insane Clown Posse (I.C.P.), you need to know that, according to VH1.com they are, "a cartoonish metal/rap band with a vaunted live show that features open fires, chainsaws, liters of soda dousing the audience (Faygo being the group's favorite brand), and more emphasis on performance art than the performance of music."

The other thing you need to know is that some authorities regard I.C.P. with a very jaundiced eye. This was made clear to 14-year-old Daniel Shellhammer when he and a friend were stopped by a couple of cops in Northwood, Ohio. They were both wearing the band's Christmas T-shirt which showed Santa Claus with a bullet in his head on the front and the words, "Merry F**kin' Xmas B**ch!" on the back. The boys were told to take their shirts off. Unless they did as ordered, the officers threatened to tear the T-shirts off them and arrest them on a charge of disorderly conduct. Daniel offered a compromise solution whereby they would turn the shirts inside out. This was turned down and the police took the shirts and sent the boys on their way. Daniel decided to sue. The police tried to make out that there was some kind of ban on I.C.P. merchandise in Ohio but this was clearly not true. The shirts might not be in the best possible taste but would you really want some testosterone crazy cop stripping your kid of his shirt?

Irate Italians

Some Chicago lawyers have banded together to form the American Italian Defense Association because they have been upset by The Sopranos, the highly successful series made by

H.B.O. The lawyers allege that the portrayal of Italians in the series suggests "that criminality is in the blood or in the genes of Italian Americans and that Italians as early immigrants to this country had little opportunity other than to turn to crime."

Apparently, the AIDA is not after money nor does it seek to have the show taken off. Their aim is to get a judgment that the show offends the dignity of Italian Americans. H.B.O. are not impressed and have issued a statement saying, they are "very proud of The Sopranos. We're hardly alone in our assessment that the show is an extraordinary artistic achievement."

Irish and irresponsible

In these days of political correctness, you would think long and hard before referring in public to any offensive national stereotypes (except about the French, of course). Would you call Swedes morose, Italians greasy and dishonest, or Germans authoritarian and humorless? No, not if you wanted to keep out of trouble. This makes what follows seem very strange indeed. A woman from Orlando, Florida, had an Irish boyfriend who was on holiday in the U.S. He hired a car and they went together to see the sights. The boyfriend then got drunk, crashed the car, and the woman was killed. The driver was arrested and charged with manslaughter and drunk driving. The woman's relatives then filed suit against the car rental company. Would you like to guess on what grounds? The company "either knew or should have known about the unique cultural and ethnic customs in Ireland which involve the regular consumption of alcohol at pubs as a major component to Irish social life." Or, to put it another way, the Irish are a bunch of drunks. Which just shows that even political correctness has its work cut out to dissuade people from starting loony lawsuits.

Its knot my fawlt I carnt spel

There must be only one thing worse than having an ugly, tasteless tattoo disfiguring your body and that is to have one that is incorrectly spelt. This is what happened to Lee Williams who sued a tattoo parlor for $47,500 over the misspelling of the word "villain." The tattooist was indignant at being sued and pointed out that it was Williams himself who had chosen the spelling. Apparently, neither of them had been too sure exactly what the right form of the word was and, after much debate, had settled for the wrong one. What is even more bizarre is that Williams had worn the tattoo for years without realizing the mistake, until a friend spotted the error and teased him about it.

He claimed that it cost $1,900 to have the thing removed. The most delicious irony of the whole affair is that the original report of the case was carried in a newspaper called The Sacramento Bee. Spelling? Bee? You can't help but laugh.

Make sense of this one!

In 1997, a SilkAir plane crashed in Indonesia with loss of life. The families of three of the victims filed lawsuits and, thanks to a Los Angeles jury, an award was made of $43.6 million.

The interesting bit is this: the jury decided that the crash was caused by defects in the rudder control system and therefore held that the firm that manufactured the hydraulic equipment was to blame. However, the crash had been investigated by the U.S. National Transportation Safety Board and they found that there were no mechanical defects on the plane. Their conclusion was that the pilot had deliberately flown the plane into the ground. Unfortunately for the defendants, under federal law NTSB reports are not admissible as evidence in a trial so the manufacturer will now have to appeal.

Milk mayhem?

The events of September 11, 2001, and other related terrorist incidents have combined to make airport authorities more suspicious and vigilant. Sometimes, the results have been unexpected and just a tad absurd.

For example, a woman was stopped and searched by a security guard who found that she was carrying three bottles of an unidentified white liquid. Could it be ricin? Or anthrax maybe? Or even a new form of plague virus? The woman insisted that it was simply mother's milk that she had expressed ready to feed her baby. The guard was not convinced and ordered her to take a sip from each bottle. She offered to sprinkle a little on her wrist and lick it off but he wasn't satisfied. So, in the end, she gave in and took three sips. As she didn't keel over and die, he assumed that she had been telling the truth (although it didn't occur to him that she might die later). The woman was hopping mad about the whole incident and decided to sue. Her lawyer was withering about the whole incident. "I'm all for random searches" he said, "but I think the number of Caucasian lactating mothers who have passed through al-Qaida training camps is negligible." Now, that may well be true, but of course Osama bin Laden and his followers are as capable of hearing the news as the rest of us. So now that they've been given the idea...

Slippery suit

Alvin Laskin ran a nursery (the sort where you grow flowers rather than kids) but, sadly for him, business was not booming. In fact, things were so bad that he had to look around for an alternative way to make a living. The ingenuity of the human mind never fails to amaze. Alvin came up with a real bobby-dazzler of an idea: he would re-sell old oil. Yes, that nasty dirty stuff that comes out of your car and is hell to get rid of.

Alvin cast his net wide and was soon taking large quantities of oil from factories and then selling it on for a variety of purposes, such as dust control. However, Alvin was not the most ecologically aware of citizens. He was storing hundreds of thousands of gallons of the stuff in leaky, corroded tanks, and even in ponds. Ugh!

Eventually, officials in Ohio started to investigate Alvin's dirty deeds and found that he was the proud owner of a huge amount of chemical sludge that contained all sorts of toxic goodies such as lead, dioxin, and PCBs. The authorities were not best pleased when their experts told them that it would cost over $30 million to clean the site up and make sure that no toxins leaked into groundwater.

The job of doing the clean-up fell to the Environmental Protection Agency and their first thought was to get the necessary cash out of Alvin. However, they soon discovered that he had no money. Undaunted, they decided to sue some of his best customers. These were big companies that had sold him oil or bought it from him. That sounded like a promising course of action, but it started to get complicated when the large companies decided to sue the other companies (over 600 of them!) who had also had dealings with Alvin's dirty oil business. Now it gets really wild. The big companies also decided to sue each other and some of them sued their insurers. Eventually, there was so much suing going on, that the city of Cleveland, Ohio, ran out of lawyers to take care of all the new business. Do you want to know how long all this took? Well, it started in the early 1970s and latest reports suggest that not all the cases are settled even now.

Taking it to the top

It is quite usual in legal cases for those dissatisfied with the outcome to appeal. But not many of them take the unusual step of suing God. Yet this is exactly what a Pennsylvania man tried to do. Over 30 years ago, he was employed by the U.S.X. Corporation and they fired him. This, he claims, ruined his life. He has attempted to sue God for failing to take "corrective action" against those who have wronged him. He also wants God to compensate him by granting him another go at being young and, this time around, giving him the ability to play the guitar. You will be less than surprised to hear that his claims are not getting far in the courts.

Telephone trial

What do personal injury lawyers get up to when they aren't busy suing on behalf of their clients? They sue on their own behalf, of course!

Harvey W. Daniels is a personal injury lawyer with a practice in Monroeville, Pennsylvania. Obviously he had too much time on his hands and came up with a way to put his credentials to use: he sued his local telephone directory because he didn't like his ads. Why? Well, the ads didn't say that he was a personal injury lawyer and the photo used was "so grotesque that the plaintiff looked like an albino and discouraged any client from contacting him." It seemed that Mr. Daniel chose not to read the proofs of his ads before they were published but, even so, he believed that blame was attached to the directory's publisher. He said, "My fellow lawyers tease me about it. What potential client would call me looking like that?" He reckoned the ugly photo should get $500,000 in punitive damages and compensation.

The fax of the case

When Hooters restaurant chain used a fax service to advertise its services, they were unaware of the effect they would have on lawyer Sam Nicholson. He was so annoyed at the faxes he received that he looked into the matter and found that Congress had banned "junk faxes." He started a class action against Hooters. The jury found the restaurant chain guilty of sending half a dozen faxes to over 1,300 class members. The judge set damages at nearly $12 million, with $6,000 for each plaintiff and $4 million for their lawyers.

The naked truth

The New York Times carried an intriguing report on the 2001 Mermaid Parade. It seems that one woman took the spirit of celebration a tad too far when she appeared wearing nothing but a thong and body paint. She caught the eye of the police who promptly arrested her for exposure. For some reason, she waited a whole year before filing a lawsuit against the city and the police officer who stopped her. Her lawyer was quoted as saying that she filed the suit as a "precautionary note not to spoil this year's parade."

Ticket trauma

Have you ever taken the kids to one of those recreation centers where they can win vouchers and eventually claim a prize? Suppose you went and your kid was given less vouchers than you thought he was entitled to. What would you do? Complain to the manager perhaps?

According to Florida's Sun-Sentinel, one father, Chris Fillichio, got really angry when his son was short changed by the prize redemption machine. Instead of giving the kid the 1,000 tickets he was entitled to, it issued a mere 150. Mr. Fillichio became so angry that he was asked to leave the recreation center. Naturally, he sued. He claimed that his son was "traumatized, began uncontrollably crying" and was afraid to hold his next birthday party at the center. Taking a case like that to the small claims court might seem a bit excessive but Mr. Fillichio's lawyer is not stopping there—he wants to go to a higher court and get the case recognized as a class action on behalf of all the poor children who have been so shamefully treated there.

Trouble with tape

Customers at the post office in Fulton, Missouri, will find themselves in a sticky situation if they try to wrap up parcels on the premises. There is no tape. Why? Because a customer hurt himself while using the tape dispenser and filed a claim against the U.S. Postal Service. As a result, the tape machine has been removed.

Unable to switch off

The family of Timothy Dumouchel of West Bend, Wisconsin, became so addicted to cable TV that he threatened to sue the provider Charter Communications. According to the plaintiff, TV was responsible for his wife's weight gain and for his kids turning into couch potatoes. He threatened to sue the cable company. Dumouchel wanted $5,000 or three computers, plus a lifetime supply of free Internet service from Charter Communications to settle his claim.

Dumouchel told Charter staff that he planned to sue because, though he repeatedly tried to get his cable connection canceled, it remained intact for four years. The result was that he and his family got free cable from August of 1999 to December 23, 2003. "I believe that the reason I smoke and drink every day and my wife is overweight is because we watched TV every day for the last four years," he complained. He continued, "But the reason I am suing Charter is they did not let me make a decision as to what was best for myself and my family and [they have been] keeping cable [coming] into my home for four years after I asked them to turn it off."

Underpass

In case you don't know it, the South Padre Island Causeway is a low bridge. This raises a number of important concerns like, would it really be a good idea to try to fly underneath the bridge? On the whole, you'd have to say it was an unwise plan. However, two fliers decided to go up in a small plane and do just that. Their fast pass was a blazing success, straight under the bridge with no trouble at all. Emboldened by success they decided to have another go. Bang! Wipeout! Autopsies on the two bodies showed evidence of illegal drugs in their bloodstreams. Their families are now suing on the grounds that the city, or the airport, should have done something to check that the two were fit to fly. Experience teaches though that when someone decides to be an idiot, there is little you can do to stop him.

Watching him die

Snowmobiles can be a lot of fun but they also have their dangers. It's not that unusual to come off and end up with the machine on top of you. What is unusual is for a snowmobile to be involved in a collision with a car. This, however, is exactly what happened to one woman driver. She struck a snowmobile and fatally injured the driver. The police were called and established that the snowmobile had cut in front of the woman's car and that she was at fault in no way. You might think that she'd thank her lucky stars that she was not the one to die. But no, she decided to sue the man's widow to get compensation for the psychological injuries she endured as she watched the man die.

Willy win?

The music business is notoriously hard to crack. Sheer talent is not always enough. This was certainly the case for Santiago Durango. He had spent years lugging his guitar around and had little to show for his trouble. He had no home of his own, was always broke, and could only afford a rusty old car. What should he do? The answer, of course, was to go to law school. "Who's ever heard of a poor lawyer?" he probably thought to himself. Once he was qualified the money didn't exactly roll in but he still had high hopes. One evening at a party, he was dead drunk when someone introduced him to Cynthia Plaster Caster—a lady who is famous for her plaster casts of celebrities' genitals. She told him a sad tale of how her manager had somehow got his hands on her collection of penis casts. In a drunken state, Santiago vowed to use the might of the law to recover the stolen penis casts. When he sobered up, he felt obliged to keep his word so he sued and won.

Clowning around

A clown without a custard pie is as unimaginable as Laurel without Hardy or Rogers without Hammerstein. Even so, there is a possibility that throwing custard pies may soon be a thing of the past. During a recent convention held by Clowns International, the assembled funny men were advised to take out custard pie insurance in case a member of the audience should be less than thrilled at getting a pie in the face. It is feared that it will not be long before clowns join the long list of those being sued for personal injury. However, Martin "Zippo" Burton, who is V.P. of Clowns International, is taking a robust approach to the problem and has been quoted as saying, "If you are stupid enough to sit in the front row, then you deserve it. It's a sad world if clowns can't be clowns."

Burning ambition

A couple of guys in Alpena, Michigan, were having financial trouble with the store they ran together, so they decided to set light to it and grab the insurance money. What they wanted was a small fire that would look convincing and make lots of smoke that would damage their stock beyond recovery. What they got was a small inferno that quickly spread to the store next door. What did they do? You must be getting the hang of how these stories work by now. Yes, that's right, they sued the insurance company. Why? On the grounds that the damage to the neighboring store was accidental and they were therefore entitled to a payout. When the case first went to trial, their claim was thrown out. However, at the Court of Appeals they had better luck and won. Eventually, the matter came before the Michigan Supreme Court where the case was thrown out.

Mad move

A man living in Metz, France, decided that his apartment was no longer big enough, so he had a bright idea. While his neighbor was at work, he knocked down the wall that separated the two apartments and moved in. When the rightful owner came back, he found his neighbor in the kitchen cooking dinner. The owner tried to get his unwelcome guest to leave but he refused. The police were called and the interloper tried to persuade them that the enlarged apartment (complete with smashed wall) was his.

He might have got away with it, had he not added that he was a pharaoh and lived in a labyrinth within a pyramid. The neighbor's attempts to sue for compensation were hampered by the fact that the man became a long-stay guest at the local psychiatric hospital.

Doctor's debts

Kelsey McMillan, aged 35, had a really bright idea for easy living. She conned her way into a British air force base by pretending to be an army medic on a training course. She lived there for five months undetected. She ran up a hefty bar bill and even managed to travel on Royal Air Force helicopters which were taking part in search and rescue operations. It was only when she applied for transfer to another base that anyone realized she was a fraud. The RAF was faced with the task of trying to reclaim the cost of her extended vacation.

Lottery loss

Some lawsuits are just so bizarre, you can't imagine how the people who filed them ever imagined they would get away with it. For example, a woman from Ohio claimed that she had won $162 million in a lottery but that she had lost her ticket. She sued the organizers of the lottery in the hope that she would be awarded the jackpot. Later on, however, reality kicked in, and she was forced to withdraw the case and admit she had lied. She said that she had bought a ticket and lost it but it was not the winning one. She claimed that her desire to help her family was what prompted the fraud. The thing that makes your brain ache is that she ever imagined that anyone would hand her that much money on such a flimsy pretext.

Woman trouble

There are two lawsuit stories that do the rounds and have been believed by thousands. The first is about a woman who bought a contraceptive gel and then sued the manufacturer because it didn't work. On investigation, they found she had been taking the stuff orally. This may be funny but it isn't true.

Another urban myth involves a woman who sued the makers of her regular brand of tampons on the grounds that she had used them for several years but was still unable to swim, play tennis, or ride a horse. Ha, ha—but again, not true.

Fiat feat

When Steve Lucas, a British law student, was stopped by police and accused of driving his Fiat Punto at 115 mph in a 70 mph zone, he was frankly incredulous. If convicted he would get a heavy fine and lose his driving license. The Punto is a small hatchback and is popular as a runabout but hardly rates as a high speed machine. Steve was happy to admit that he'd been doing 85 mph and pay the fine but he insisted that his car simply wasn't capable of going any faster. Eventually, he hired an independent expert to drive his car round a race track to prove his point. The police had to stop their case when the expert's report backed up Steve's claim. They settled for fining him £40 ($75) for driving without due care and attention.